Books by Delmore Schwartz

T0275518

Portrait of Delmore (ed. Pollet), 1͘

The Ego Is Always at the Wheel (ed. Phillips), 1986

Letters (ed. Phillips), 1985

Last and Lost Poems (ed. Phillips), 1979

In Dreams Begin Responsibilities: Eight Stories (ed. Atlas), 1978

What Is To Be Given: Selected Poems of Delmore Schwartz, (ed. Dunn), 1976

Selected Essays of Delmore Schwartz (ed. Dike & Zucker), 1970

Selected Poems (1938–1958): Summer Knowledge (reprint), 1967

Syracuse Poems 1964 (Selected and with a Foreword by Delmore Schwartz), 1965

Successful Love and Other Stories, 1961

Summer Knowledge: New and Selected Poems, 1959

Vaudeville for a Princess and Other Poems, 1950

The World Is a Wedding (stories), 1948

Genesis: Book I, 1943

Shenandoah (verse play), 1941

A Season in Hell (translation), 1939; revised second edition, 1940

In Dreams Begin Responsibilities (poems and stories), 1938

When I remember the advent of the dazzling beauty

As it descended, sudden and unknown

I turn again to stiffened stone, along
                 the
        With poverty of   having known the dazzling
                of beauty,

    But only as a memory is known; only as a lake,
                a weekend or midnight
                    streaming
        Know the glory   the great blue heights

            riding in a storm of white disorder,
        Of the cavalry of Aurora Borealis.

Last & Lost Poems

DELMORE SCHWARTZ

EDITED WITH AN
INTRODUCTION BY
ROBERT PHILLIPS

A NEW DIRECTIONS BOOK

Originally published in 1979 by Vanguard Press. Published in a revised edition as New Directions Paperbook 673 in 1989 Published simultaneously in Canada by Penguin Books Canada Limited

Library of Congress Cataloging-in-Publication Data
Schwartz, Delmore, 1913–1966. Last & lost poems.
Rev. ed. of: Last and lost poems of Delmore Schwartz. 1979.
I. Phillips, Robert S.   II. Schwartz, Delmore, 1913–1966.
Last and lost poems of Delmore Schwartz.   III. Title.
PS3537.C79A6   1989   811'.52   88-31396
ISBN 0-8112-1096-0

New Directions Books are published for James Laughlin
by New Directions Publishing Corporation,
80 Eighth Avenue, New York 10011

Third Printing

Acknowledgments

Thanks are due to Amy S. Doherty, University Archivist, George Arents Research Library at Syracuse University; to Judith A. Schiff, Chief Research Archivist, Manuscripts and Archives, Sterling Memorial Library, Yale University; to Donald C. Gallup of the Collection of American Literature, Beinecke Rare Book and Manuscript Library; to Kenneth A. Schwartz, the poet's brother and heir; and to Dwight Macdonald, literary executor for the Estate of Delmore Schwartz, for his help in facilitating publication.

Grateful acknowledgment is also made to the following for permission to reprint previously uncollected poems, a number of which I placed with quarterlies after the poet's death:

Commentary, for "Poem" and "Sonnet," copyright © 1958 by The American Jewish Committee.
Kenyon Review, for "Journey of a Poem Compared to All the Sad Variety of Travel," copyright 1962, by Kenyon College.
New Directions in Prose and Poetry, for "Metro-Goldwyn-Mayer," copyright 1937 by New Directions Publishing Corporation; and for "Paris and Helen," copyright 1941 by New Directions Publishing Corporation.
The New Republic, for "Kilroy's Carnival: A Poetic Prologue for TV," "The Choir and Music of Solitude and Silence," "Spiders," "All Night, All Night," "This is a Poem I Wrote at Night Before the Dawn," "Words for a Trumpet Chorale Celebrating the Autumn," "Aria [from Kilroy's Carnival]," and "Remember Midsummer: The Fragrance of Box, of White Roses," reprinted by permission of *The New Republic*, © 1958, 1959, 1961, 1962, 1968, *The New Republic*.
The New York Times, for "The First Night of Fall and Falling Rain," "Poem: In the morning, when it was raining," and "To Helen (after Valéry)," © 1962 by The New York Times Company. Reprinted by permission.
The Ontario Review, for passages from "The Studies of Narcissus," copyright © 1976, *The Ontario Review*.
Partisan Review, for "Love and Marilyn Monroe," copyright © 1976 by P.R., Inc.

Poetry, for "Poem: Old man in the crystal morning after snow," "Poem: You, my photographer," and for "Apollo Musagete, Poetry, and the Leader of the Muses," © 1937, 1937, 1962 by Modern Poetry Association.

Prairie Schooner, for "Philology Recapitulates Ontology, Poetry is Ontology" and "Poem," © 1959, University of Nebraska Press.

Sewanee Review, for "Two Lyrics from Kilroy's Carnival: a Masque," © 1961, The University of the South.

Southern Review, for two sections from "The Studies of Narcissus" and "Phoenix Lyrics," copyright 1976 by Louisiana State University; for three sections from "The Studies of Narcissus," copyright 1977 by Louisiana State University.

Thanks also to Kenneth A. Schwartz for permission to print "What Curious Dresses All Men Wear," from an article by Dwight Macdonald in *The New York Review of Books* (Sept. 8, 1966).

My wife, Judith Bloomingdale, helped decipher difficult manuscripts. My editor, Bernice Woll, has again proven herself to be an editor's editor. And I especially wish to acknowledge the encouragement and friendship of Frank Peter Piskor.

CONTENTS

Foreword

This book is intended as a rescue mission — putting into print some late and uncollected work by Delmore Schwartz, a man whom many consider one of this century's most important American poets. A portion of the book publishes for the first time works found among the dead poet's papers.

It should be recorded that it is just short of a miracle that *any* Schwartz papers survive. The story is worth telling: Of the nine cartons at Yale University, six are early papers, recovered by Schwartz's literary executor, Dwight Macdonald, in an extraordinary sequence of circumstances. When Schwartz left Manhattan for his teaching post at Syracuse University in 1962, he abandoned all his early manuscripts and letters in his Greenwich Village apartment. The moving man who was summoned by the landlord to dispose of the room's contents knew and liked Schwartz from evenings drinking together at the White Horse Tavern. He recognized the apartment's contents as Schwartz material, and instead of disposing of all manuscripts, as hired to do, stored them at his own expense. Years later, after Schwartz's death, he found himself bending elbows in another Village bar with Dwight Macdonald's son. "Your father's a literary man," he said. "Do you think he'd be interested in Delmore Schwartz manuscripts? I've got boxes of them." The younger Macdonald said he thought his father would be. The six boxes came out of storage and went to Dwight Macdonald, who, as literary executor of the estate, supervised their transfer to Yale. They are now in the collection of American Literature, Beinecke Rare Book and Manuscript Library, at Yale.

Another coincidence accounts for the survival of papers from Schwartz's last year. After fleeing Syracuse for the last time in January 1966, he lived in the Columbia Hotel near Broadway, where, in July of that year, he died. When the body was removed to the city morgue, it was unclaimed for some days — a fact noted in *The New York Times*. Reading this, Macdonald walked over to the hotel, identified himself as a friend of the deceased, and asked at the desk if there was anything he could do. "We're cleaning out his room this very minute," the manager told him. "Take anything you want." Macdonald rushed upstairs and scooped up the remaining three cartons of papers housed at Yale. It is sad to relate that no poems of value were found in those cartons, but other papers and memorabilia help fill in the story of his last days.

As for the papers at Syracuse University, there is still some mystery surrounding how they got there. Even the University archivist is uncertain of their origins. Some of the material dates from Schwartz's years at Syracuse, much is considerably earlier. The poet's brother, Kenneth, believes they were left in storage at Syracuse by Schwartz just before he left for New York the last time. Those papers are slated to be transferred to Yale shortly, to form one vast Schwartz collection in the Beinecke.

Why collect, and publish, Schwartz's last and unpublished works? For the simple reason that he was, in the minds of many, a major American poet. As Allen Tate said of Schwartz's first collection, [*In Dreams Begin Responsibilities*] published in 1938 when the poet was only twenty-four, "Schwartz's poetic style is the only genuine innovation we've had since Pound and Eliot came upon the scene twenty-five years ago. In his verse there is a wholly new feeling for language and in the regular versification a new metrical system of great subtlety and originality." And from John Crowe Ransom: "He has a natural command of the poetic language, and that is what few poets have today, even the noted ones. You do not take his lines apart and see how they are made. He has the gift of the fused, indivisible poetic style."

But Schwartz was widely read for three decades for more reasons than his style and versification. Subject matter also had a great deal to do with his success. With a Depression just behind America, and a second World War just ahead, Schwartz was a poet of major conflicts and changes, of the individual in conflict with Time and the times. "No young poet, perhaps no poet of the period, has so skillfully registered the threat of change and the cruelty of time," Louis Untermeyer wrote.

Schwartz's early, rather Yeatsian poems — such as "For the One Who Would Take Man's Life in His Hands" and "The Heavy Bear Who Goes with Me" — were most often concerned with divisions, those within the poet's own consciousness and those in the exterior world around him. Much of his education included the study of philosophy, and his early poems were philosophically oriented. Delmore Schwartz's poems made people think.

After his early bravura performance, Schwartz spent the rest of his life trying to exceed himself. "I'd bleed to say his lovely work improved/but it is not so," John Berryman wrote in one of his eleven *Dream Songs* dedicated to Delmore Schwartz's memory. His poetry did not, in fact, "improve." It became different. Few readers have been willing to examine these differences, to find merit in the later work. Not many have been willing to agree with William Barrett, writing in *Commentary* of September 1974, "Delmore had a beautiful lyrical talent, and so long as he continued able to write anything at all, this gift doesn't seem to have left him."

No: "Poor Delmore," the myth goes, "he was bright, then burned out like a candle." This is the popular portrait of Schwartz perpetrated in Saul Bellow's roman à clef, *Humboldt's Gift*, and in James Atlas's *Delmore Schwartz: The*

Life of An American Poet. Mr. Atlas quotes, for instance, from Schwartz's "Darkling Summer, Ominous Dusk, Rumorous Rain," which Schwartz wrote in 1958 — a fairly late poem in his career. It begins,

> A tattering of rain and then the reign
> Of pour and pouring-down and down,
> Where in the westwind gathered and filming gown
> Of grey and clouding weakness, and, in the mane
> Of the light's glory and the day's splendor, gold and
>   vain,
> Vivid, more and more vivid, scarlet, lucid and more
>   luminous,
> Then came a splatter, a prattle, a blowing rain!
> And soon the hour was musical and rumorous:
> A softness of a dripping lipped the isolated house —
> A gaunt grey somber softness licked the glass of
>   hours . . . .

Mr. Atlas labels this stanza an example of "haphazard, euphonious, virtually incomprehensible effusions . . .," one of many "empty symphonies of sound" that "verge on being devoid of any sense whatever."

I disagree. This poem — and many others dating from Schwartz's last decade — differs from his early work in that it clearly is not an attempt to mythologize himself, or to dramatize history, or to pay homage to the world of culture. Rather, it often accurately re-creates a sensuous experience and does so in language that is musical, free-associative, and highly communicative: "a splatter, a prattle, a blowing rain!" It is an example of his later style of spontaneous effusion, characterized by energy and delight (two qualities cited and approved by Douglas Dunn in his excellent introduction to an English edition of selected Schwartz poems, *What Is To Be Given*). To dismiss such poems because of their euphony would be to dismiss Gerard Manley Hopkins, Dame Edith Sitwell, and Dylan Thomas, to name three.

With their accumulations of details and syntactical repetitions, Schwartz's late poems seem to be modeled after Whitman rather than his early master, Yeats. Indeed, the title of one late poem begins, "A Dream of Whitman, Paraphrased. . . ." Schwartz's poems from the fifties and early sixties are written in longer lines, with more relaxed syntax and more apparent good humor. They mark an enormous stylistic change of direction from such early stripped-bare works as "In the Naked Bed, in Plato's Cave" or "The Ballad of the Children of the Czar." In the later work, as has been remarked by the editors of the *Norton Anthology of Modern Poetry*, "The poet now hopes — prays, even, since the poems are often beseeching — that he can settle his argument with himself by substituting for the warfare of philosophical concepts the healing rhythms of nature," a nature which holds out the promise that,

> You
> Were what you are not now, now you are what you
>   were not, and you are
> Open and ever-ripening and far less than what you may
>   become or be
> Within the future's bewildering reality.

Schwartz chose to include more than a hundred of such late poems in his selected volume, *Summer Knowledge* (published in 1959 and reprinted in 1967 under the title *Selected Poems: Summer Knowledge*). This is one reason the present book is not longer. In the best of the late poems gathered in that volume, Schwartz is not unlike Vivaldi in *The Seasons* — celebrating the joys and vigors, enervations and languishments of the world's weathers. (The comparison is not far-fetched: one of Schwartz's later and longer poems is titled simply "Vivaldi." He was always aware of the relationship between musical and poetic forms; his first book contained a sequence subtitled, "Eleven Poems in Imitation of the Fugue Form.") And in the best of the late work, as in "During December's Death," Schwartz's imagery yields to strong statement, repudiating Atlas's charge of "empty symphonies of sound":

> *Wait: wait: wait as if you had always waited*
> *And as if it had always been dark*
> *And as if the world had been from the beginning*
> *A lost and drunken ark in which the only light*
> *Was the dread and white of the terrified animals'*
>   *eyes. . . .*

[The italics are Schwartz's.]

Another "myth" concerning Schwartz is the notion that he wrote little or nothing in his later years. One would think the inclusion of those hundred pages of new work in *Summer Knowledge* would have dispelled the notion. That was in 1959. Even in his difficult, tormented final years, spent largely at Syracuse University, where I was privileged to know him, Schwartz was more productive than most supposed. He was working largely in prose. A number of his colleagues in the English Department at Syracuse read the manuscripts of new short stories, from a collection to be titled *A Child's Universal History.* That manuscript seems to have vanished. He also produced a number of poems from a sequence he titled "Kilroy's Carnival: A Masque," several of which appeared in quarterlies and are reprinted here for the first time in a book. Their relation to his "Poetic Prologue for TV" of the same name is not clear.

Schwartz prepared no new book of poems for publication in the eight years of life left him following *Summer Knowledge.* Had he lived longer, presumably he would have. In those of his papers presently housed at Syracuse University, I found two different tables of contents of poems Schwartz had drawn up at separate times in the 1960s. Many of the poems included in the present volume were among those he planned to collect.

This would appear to contradict Donald A. Dike and David H. Zucker, in their preface to *Selected Essays of Delmore Schwartz*, who depict Schwartz in his last years as showing little interest in the act or fact of publication, his life so occupied with writing and with the mental illness that ultimately consumed him that "The publication of a book was unimportant, a trivial irrelevance." This attitude agrees, surely, with Schwartz's statement, posited in his 1949 essay, "Views of a Second Violinist," that "I've decided that one ought to write as much as possible and publish as little as possible." Still, Schwartz was submitting the most finished of his poems to quarterlies and to the editorial page of *The New York Times* (for a quick twenty-five dollars), which in those days published poetry. He continued to do so at least into the autumn of 1962.

II

Last and Lost Poems of Delmore Schwartz attempts to bring together all those poems Schwartz wrote after his last collection was published and that, in every probability, he would have included in his sixth, had he lived to put together such a volume. Here are all the poems Schwartz completed and offered for individual publication in magazines, newspapers, and anthologies between 1958 and his death on July 11, 1966. Also included are a number of late, unpublished, but clearly completed poems (as complete as any poem ever is: as Valéry states, "A poem is never finished, merely abandoned"). These include the tributes to Whitman, Joyce, Frost, Einstein, and Marilyn Monroe, "News of the Gold World of May," "America, America!", the "Phoenix Poems," several of the poems on poetry, two Valéry translations, and three Rilke translations. Most were found in the poet's papers at Syracuse.

Some predate Schwartz's last collection by a year or more. In all probability they were among the then-new poems he sacrificed from *Summer Knowledge* to make way for older poems, at the suggestion of his Doubleday editor, Jason Epstein. Doubleday recently had published Theodore Roethke's new and selected volume, *Words for the Wind*, and in a letter (now at the Beinecke) to Schwartz, Epstein urged the same format upon him. The scheme was changed, in 1959, from one of all-new works to one of "New and Selected Poems," and certain of the new poems had to go. Among the casualties was almost all of the long "Studies of Narcissus," only three sections of which were included in *Summer Knowledge* ("The Mind is an Ancient and Famous Capital," "The Fear and Dream of the Mind of the Others," and "The River Was the Emblem of All Beauty: All"). "The Studies of Narcissus" is published in its entirety here for the first time. The typescript, found in the Beinecke papers, is thirty pages long, clearly unfinished, but frequently brilliant. It was, in all probability, Schwartz's last attempt at a "major" poem after the failure of *Genesis: Books II and III*.

Also published here for the first time is a much longer version of "Kilroy's Carnival, a Poetic Prologue for Television." The original version was cut considerably either by Schwartz or the editor of *The New Republic* when it appeared in that magazine. Schwartz was anxious to see it in print, as his letters to several editors indicate, and perhaps bent to space requirements.

I have also decided to include a few earlier poems published in magazines in the poet's lifetime, but that also have remained uncollected. These include poems he published in *Poetry*, *Commentary*, and two of the *New Directions in Prose and Poetry* annuals. In the Schwartz canon they seem representative of his early work. Several document his fascination with film, Hollywood, and his debt to Baudelaire

("You hypocrite! My brother! We are a pair!"). His best and most famous short story, "In Dreams Begin Responsibilities," utilizes the device of the hero's dreams projected as an old movie, and it is interesting to trace images of films in his poems from "Metro-Goldwyn-Mayer" (1937) to whimsical casting suggestions for "Paris and Helen" (1941) up to "Love and Marilyn Monroe" (1955).

A word about "Paris and Helen": Schwartz published it in the New Directions annual for 1941, but — unlike two other verse plays, *Shenandoah* and "Dr. Bergen's Belief" — it never received book publication with his poems. While it lacks the depth of *Shenandoah,* it should not be lost. (On the other hand, a fourth and very early Schwartz play, "Choosing Company," can be found in the *New Caravan* anthology of 1936. While very gifted, it is in some ways juvenile. It contains some wonderful passages of irony and humor, but its formalistic structure is somewhat pretentious, and, as James Laughlin [Schwartz's New Directions editor] stated in a letter to me, there is difficulty "in relating the 'philosophical' abstract passages of poetry which some of the characters speak to the actual, rather concrete and forceful subject of the play." Schwartz's reputation and this particular collection would not benefit from reprinting it. It is also one of the earliest works Schwartz published, whereas my primary emphasis has been upon the latest. (Other juvenilia I have not included are the poems "Automobile," "Darkness," "E.A.P. — A Portrait," and "The Saxophone," from *The Poet's Pack of George Washington High School* [1931], and "Aubade" from *Mosaic,* I [1934].)

One poem that may be completely unknown is "What Curious Dresses All Men Wear." It is a short lyric Schwartz wrote in the copy of his first book he gave to his friend, Dwight Macdonald. At Macdonald's instigation it has been anthologized at least once, by William Cole, but it has never appeared in a book by Schwartz himself. Perhaps Schwartz considered it too brief to be worthy. I have included three other brief, "occasional" poems, all unpublished. While not great poetry, they delight.

I have necessarily made several editorial decisions, choosing from a number of variant versions of various poems. For example, Schwartz published one, "Aria," said to be from "Kilroy's Carnival: a Masque," in three different magazines in slightly different versions. When more than one version exists, I have chosen the latest. I have left the simple title "Poem" on all those pieces so designated by Schwartz, but have included the first line of each in the Table of Contents for easy identification. I decided against publishing manuscripts of shorter poems when Schwartz himself had included them, or portions of them, in longer sequences. The longer is invariably the later version. For instance, the charming "Poems on that Day of Summer, Blue and Gold" (*The New Republic*, Oct. 19, 1959) was reworked and incorporated into the longer "May's Truth and May's Falsehood" (*Summer Knowledge*). I have dated each poem where possible. Some dates are educated guesses, and as such are followed by question marks.

This book, then, contains over forty pieces, only seven of which were not written during the 1950s and '60s. "Verse is pouring out of my fingers," Atlas quotes Schwartz announcing to Clement Greenberg one day in the late fifties. Over a quarter of them were written in 1962, which appears to have been a very good year for his poetic productivity. It was also the year in which Schwartz saw the last of his poems to be published in his lifetime ("The First Night of Fall and Falling Rain" appeared in *The New York Times* on November 6 of that year).

There is, it should be said, an incredible amount of unpublished *early* poetry by Schwartz. Lila Lee Valenti has made an initial study of the drafts and revisions of Schwartz's earliest poems. Her essay, "The Apprenticeship of Delmore Schwartz," published in *Twentieth-Century Literature*, reveals Schwartz's quick and thorough mastery of the genres in which he was to work — a mastery so facile that his *Vaudeville for a Princess* (1950) includes a sequence of forty sonnets, only one of which he later thought good enough to reprint in *Summer Knowledge*. Of the earlier, unpublished sonnets, Ms. Valenti publishes fifteen within her essay.

The monolithic manuscript of *Genesis: Book II* also remains. (*Book I* was published by New Directions in 1943, and was not well-received.) At Syracuse are hundreds of typescript pages continuing Schwartz's long autobiographical poem. But this failed epic dates from the 1940s. James Atlas has resurrected some fascinating passages that were published in *New Directions 35* (1977).

Also yet to be dealt with are Schwartz's verse journals, dating from the early 1940s. Selections can be found in *New Directions 36* (1978).

These are but a number of projects that await the scholar at Yale and Syracuse. I have not mentioned the drafts of novels and cycles of related stories and books of criticism in manuscript. The Beinecke collection, at the time of my visit, totaled nine large boxes, the Syracuse collection, eleven.

III

These last and "lost" poems all evidence Schwartz's highly individual talent, and, I maintain, some reveal the poet was working better in his troubled last years than many have assumed. Some of them are even remarkable — especially "Spiders," "All Night, All Night," "Apollo Musagete," certain sections of "Narcissus," and the superb "To Helen" translation. I'm certain they are more mature, more interesting than much American poetry published in recent years: a poem by Frank O'Hara, parodying Schwartz's most famous title (which Schwartz himself had borrowed from an epigraph borrowed by Yeats!), illustrates the differences.

Our responsibilities did not begin
in dream, though they began in bed. Love is first of all
a lesson in utility. I hear the sewage singing
underneath my bright white toilet seat. . . .

(from *Selected Poems of Frank O'Hara*)

The lyric talent of Delmore Schwartz never celebrated utility, sewage, or the mechanics of sex. A celebrant of the intuitive rather than the analytical, of the possibilities of choice, the natural, the lovely, the beautiful, and the harmonious, Schwartz wrote poems that were, above all, refreshing and often naive. I find the same qualities in these last poems, especially those that deal with nature, poetry, and Schwartz's infatuation with film.

It is my hope that this book will send people back for another look at Schwartz's most famous poems. I observe with pleasure that the most recent reprinting of his *Selected Poems* in paperback bears the notation, "Fourth Printing." That book contains, in my opinion, some permanent contributions to twentieth-century American poetry, especially "The Ballad of the Children of the Czar," "In the Naked Bed, in Plato's Cave," "The Beautiful American Word, Sure," "A Young Child and His Pregnant Mother," "Prothalamion," "The Ballet of the Fifth Year," "Will You Perhaps Consent to Be," "The Heavy Bear Who Goes With Me," "I Am Cherry Alive," "Baudelaire," "Seurat's Sunday Afternoon Along the Seine," "Starlight Like Intuition Pierced the Twelve," and the remarkable sequence, "Coriolanus and His Mother."

Yet, as with Sylvia Plath and Anne Sexton, the legend of Delmore Schwartz's life already has begun to obfuscate the achievement of the work. So it is also my hope that the publication of *Last and Lost Poems* will help facilitate publication, someday, of a larger selection of his work. Not a *Complete Poems*, but a *Collected Poems*, perhaps — a volume that, without some of these last and ungathered works, would be incomplete and unrepresentative. From such an edition could emerge a picture of the total poetic achievement and development of the man who, at the time he received it, was the youngest American poet ever to win the prestigious Bollingen Prize, defeating in that year Robert Lowell, whose *Life Studies* had made him a likely contender.

ROBERT PHILLIPS
August 1978

Works Cited

Atlas, James. *Delmore Schwartz:* The Life of an American Poet. Farrar, Straus & Giroux, 1977.

Barrett, William. "Delmore," *Commentary,* LVIII, 3 (September 1974).

Bellow, Saul. *Humboldt's Gift.* Viking Press, 1975.

Dike, Donald A. and Zucker, David H., eds. *Selected Essays of Delmore Schwartz.* University of Chicago Press, 1970.

Dunn, Douglas. "Introduction," *What Is To Be Given*: Selected Poems of Delmore Schwartz. Carcanet New Press, 1976.

Ellman, Richard and O'Clair, Robert. *Norton Anthology of Modern Poetry.* W.W. Norton, 1973.

Untermeyer, Louis. *Modern American Poetry.* Harcourt, Brace, 1950.

Valenti, Lila Lee. "The Apprenticeship of Delmore Schwartz," *Twentieth-Century Literature,* XX, 3 (1974).

Preface to the Paperbook Edition (1989)

This is a revised version of the hardback edition published by Vanguard Press in 1979, which has just gone out of print, and copies of which can only be found in rare book shops, if they can be found at all.

In the ten years since this book's publication, Schwartz's literary stock has risen considerably, and several of the manuscripts mentioned in the original Foreword have since been published. My edition of *Letters of Delmore Schwartz* (Princeton: Ontario Review Press, 1984), and *The Ego Is Always at the Wheel: Bagatelles* (New York: New Directions, 1986), have appeared. Elizabeth Pollet's edition of the Schwartz journals and notes, 1939–1959, has been published under the title, *Portrait of Delmore* (New York: Farrar, Straus & Giroux, 1986).

Other events affecting Schwartz scholarship during this decade include the transfer from the Syracuse University Library to the Beinecke Library at Yale University of most of the Schwartz manuscripts previously held at the former institution, and the death of Schwartz's literary executor, Dwight Macdonald. Sometime after that death, I was asked to assume the responsibility for the Estate.

Since publication of *Last & Lost Poems*, I have located a number of additional unpublished poems. Of these, fifteen are now added to the original edition and seem worthy inclusions to the Schwartz canon. With the exception of "Poem to Johann Sebastian Bach" (1934), "Poem for Jacques Maritain and Leon Trotzky" (1934), "Sonnet" (1938), and the selections from *Genesis: Book II* (1940), these are poems written in the mid-to-late Fifties.

I have chosen to delete "Paris and Helen," a verse play, from this revised edition. Interested readers will find it in the forthcoming edition of all five of Schwartz's dramatic works, *Shenandoah and Other Verse Plays.*

To the original list of Acknowledgments, I wish to thank the following for permission to reprint previously unpublished and uncollected poems, which have been added to this paperback edition.

New Directions: An International Anthology of Prose & Poetry, for "Genesis: Selections from Book II," copyright © 1977 by New Directions Publishing Corporation; and for "Seven Poems," copyright © 1987 by New Directions Publishing Corporation.

Ontario Review, for "When I Remember The Advent," copyright © 1979 by Ontario Review Press.

The Paris Review, for "The Maxims of Sisyphus," "How Can He Possess," "Sonnet," "The Power and Glory of Language," "The Sequel, the Conclusion, the Endlessness," and "Poem: How Marvelous Man's Kind Is," copyright © 1986 by *The Paris Review.*

Syracuse University Library Associates Courier, for "Poem to Johann Sebastian Bach" and "Poem for Jacques Maritain and Leon Trotzky," copyright © 1985 by Syracuse University Library Associates.

Thanks also to James Atlas who originally isolated the selections from *Genesis: Book II.*

ROBERT PHILLIPS
October 1988

I

Darkness before Delight

This Is a Poem I Wrote at Night, Before the Dawn

This is a poem I wrote before I died and was reborn:
— After the years of the apples ripening and the eagles
    soaring,
After the festival here the small flowers gleamed like the
    first stars,
And the horses cantered and romped away like the
    experience of skill; mastered and serene
Power, grasped and governed by reins, lightly held by
    knowing hands.

The horses had cantered away, far enough away
So that I saw the horses' heads farther and farther away
And saw that they had reached the black horizon on the
    dusk of day
And were or seemed black thunderheads, massy and
    ominous waves in the doomed sky:
And it was then, for the first time, then that I said as I
    must always say
All through living death of night:
It is always darkness before delight!
The long night is always the beginning of the vivid
    blossom of day.

(*1961*)

3

America, America!

I am a poet of the Hudson River and the heights above it,
        the lights, the stars, and the bridges
I am also by self-appointment the laureate of the Atlantic
        — of the peoples' hearts, crossing it
            to new America.

I am burdened with the truck and chimera, hope,
        acquired in the sweating sick-excited passage
            in steerage, strange and estranged
Hence I must descry and describe the kingdom of emotion.

For I am a poet of the kindergarten (in the city)
        and the cemetery (in the city)
And rapture and ragtime and also the secret city in the
  heart and mind
This is the song of the natural city self in the 20th century.

It is true but only partly true that a city is a "tyranny of
  numbers"
(This is the chant of the urban metropolitan and
  metaphysical self
After the first two World Wars of the 20th century)

— This is the city self, looking from window to lighted
  window
When the squares and checks of faintly yellow light
Shine at night, upon a huge dim board and slab-like tombs,
Hiding many lives. It is the city consciousness
Which sees and says: more: more and more: always more.

                             (*1954*)

All Night, All Night

I have been one acquainted with the night — ROBERT FROST

Rode in the train all night, in the sick light. A bird
Flew parallel with a singular will. In daydream's moods and
  attitudes
The other passengers slumped, dozed, slept, read,
Waiting, and waiting for place to be displaced
On the exact track of safety or the rack of accident.

Looked out at the night, unable to distinguish
Lights in the towns of passage from the yellow lights
Numb on the ceiling. And the bird flew parallel and still
As the train shot forth the straight line of its whistle,
Forward on the taut tracks, piercing empty, familiar —

The bored center of this vision and condition looked and
  looked
Down through the slick pages of the magazine (seeking
The seen and the unseen) and his gaze fell down the well.
Of the great darkness under the slick glitter,
And he was only one among eight million riders and
  readers.

And all the while under his empty smile the shaking drum
Of the long determined passage passed through him
By his body mimicked and echoed. And then the train,
Like a suddenly storming rain, began to rush and thresh
The silent or passive night, pressing and impressing
The patients' foreheads with a tightening-like image
Of the rushing engine proceeded by a shaft of light
Piercing the dark, changing and transforming the silence
Into a violence of foam, sound, smoke and succession.

A bored child went to get a cup of water,
And crushed the cup because the water too was
Boring and merely boredom's struggle.
The child, returning, looked over the shoulder
Of a man reading until he annoyed the shoulder.
A fat woman yawned and felt the liquid drops
Drip down the fleece of many dinners.

And the bird flew parallel and parallel flew
The black pencil lines of telephone posts, crucified,
At regular intervals, post after post
Of thrice crossed, blue-belled, anonymous trees.

And then the bird cried as if to all of us:

> O your life, your lonely life
> What have you ever done with it,
> And done with the great gift of consciousness?
> What will you ever do with your life before death's
>   knife
> Provides the answer ultimate and appropriate?

As I for my part felt in my heart as one who falls,
Falls in a parachute, falls endlessly, and feel the vast
Draft of the abyss sucking him down and down,
An endlessly helplessly falling and appalled clown:

This is the way that night passes by, this
Is the overnight endless trip to the famous unfathomable
   abyss.

(1960)

Two Lyrics from Kilroy's Carnival:
A Masque

I *Aria*

" — Kiss me there where pride is glittering
Kiss me where I am ripened and round fruit
Kiss me wherever, however, I am supple, bare and flare
(Let the bell be rung as long as I am young:
        let ring and fly like a great bronze wing!)

" — I'll kiss you wherever you think you are poor,
Wherever you shudder, feeling striped or barred,
Because you think you are bloodless, skinny or marred:
        Until, until
        your gaze has been stilled —
Until you are shamed again no more!
I'll kiss you until your body and soul
        the mind in the body being fulfilled —
Suspend their dread and civil war!"

(*1962*)

II *Song*

Under the yellow sea
Who comes and looks with me
For the daughters of music, the fountains of poetry?
Both have soared forth from the unending waters
Where all things still are seeds and far from flowers
And since they remain chained to the sea's powers
May wilt to nonentity or loll and arise to comedy

7

Or thrown into mere accident through irrelevant incident
Dissipate all identity ceaselessly fragmented by the ocean's
    immense and intense, irresistible and insistent
    action,
Be scattered like the sand is, purposely and relentlessly,
Living in the summer resorts of the dead endlessly.

(*1962*)

Phoenix Lyrics

I

If nature is life, nature is death:
It is winter as it is spring:
Confusion is variety, variety
And confusion in everything
Make experience the true conclusion
Of all desire and opulence,
All satisfaction and poverty.

(*1957*)

II

When a hundred years had passed nature seemed to man
        a clock
Another century sank away and nature seemed a jungle
        in a rock
And now that nature has become a ticking and hidden
        bomb how we must mock
Newton, Democritus, the Deity
The heart's ingenuity and the mind's infinite
    uncontrollable
        insatiable curiosity.

(*1958*)

III

Purple black cloud at sunset: it is late August
and the light begins to look cold, and as we look,
listen and look, we hear the first drums of autumn.

(1958)

Poem

In the morning, when it was raining,
Then the birds were hectic and loudy;
Through all the reign is fall's entertaining;
Their singing was erratic and full of disorder:
They did not remember the summer blue
Or the orange of June. They did not think at all
Of the great red and bursting ball
Of the kingly sun's terror and tempest, blazing,
Once the slanting rain threw over all
The colorless curtains of the ceaseless spontaneous fall.

(*1962*)

Poem

Remember midsummer: the fragrance of box, of white
   roses
And of phlox. And upon a honeysuckle branch
Three snails hanging with infinite delicacy
— Clinging like tendril, flake and thread, as self-tormented
And self-delighted as any ballerina,
         just as in the orchard,
Near the apple trees, in the over-grown grasses
Drunken wasps clung to over-ripe pears
Which had fallen: swollen and disfigured.
For now it is wholly autumn: in the late
Afternoon as I walked toward the ridge where the hills
   begin,
There is a whir, a thrashing in the bush, and a startled
   pheasant, flying out and up,
Suddenly astonished me, breaking the waking dream.

Last night
Snatches of sleep, streaked by dreams and half dreams
— So that, aloft in the dim sky, for almost an hour,
A sausage balloon — chalk-white and lifeless looking —
   floated motionless
Until, at midnight, I went to New Bedlam and saw what I
   feared
        the most — I heard nothing, but it
        had all happened several times elsewhere.

Now, in the cold glittering morning, shining at the
   window,

The pears hang, yellowed and over-ripe, sodden brown in
         erratic places, all bunched and dangling,
Like a small choir of bagpipes, silent and waiting. And I
   rise now,
Go to the window and gaze at the fallen or falling country
— And see! — the fields are pencilled light brown
         or are the dark brownness of the last autumn
— So much has shrunken to straight brown lines, thin as
   the
         bare thin trees,
Save where the cornstalks, white bones of the lost forever
   dead,
Shrivelled and fallen, but shrill-voiced when the wind
   whistles,
Are scattered like the long abandoned hopes and ambitions
Of an adolescence which, for a very long time, has been
   merely
A recurrent target and taunt of the inescapable mockery of
   memory.

                                        (1962)

                              ·

The First Night of Fall
and Falling Rain

The common rain had come again
Slanting and colorless, pale and anonymous,
Fainting falling in the first evening
Of the first perception of the actual fall,
The long and late light had slowly gathered up
A sooty wood of clouded sky, dim and distant more and
    more
Until, at dusk, the very sense of selfhood waned,
A weakening nothing halted, diminished or denied or set
    aside,
Neither tea, nor, after an hour, whiskey,
Ice and then a pleasant glow, a burning,
And the first leaping wood fire
Since a cold night in May, too long ago to be more than
Merely a cold and vivid memory.
Staring, empty, and without thought
Beyond the rising mists of the emotion of causeless
    sadness,
How suddenly all consciousness leaped in spontaneous
    gladness;
Knowing without thinking how the falling rain (outside, all
    over)
In slow sustained consistent vibration all over outside
Tapping window, streaking roof,
            running down runnel and drain
Waking a sense, once more, of all that lived outside of us,
Beyond emotion, for beyond the swollen
            distorted shadows and lights
Of the toy town and the vanity fair
            of waking consciousness!   (1962)

14

Words for a Trumpet Chorale
Celebrating the Autumn

"The trumpet is a brilliant instrument." — DIETRICH
  BUXTEHUDE

Come and come forth and come up from the cup of
Your dumbness, stunned and numb, come with
The statues and believed in,
Thinking *this is nothing*, deceived.

      Come to the summer and sun,
      Come see upon that height, and that sum
      In the seedtime of the winter's absolute,
      How yearly the phoenix inhabits the fruit.
      Behold, above all, how the tall ball
      Called the body is but a drum, but a bell
      Summoning the soul
      To rise from the catacomb of sleep and fear
      To the blaze and death of summer,

Rising from the lithe forms of the pure
Furs of the rising flames, slender and supple,
Which are the consummation of the blaze of fall and of all.

                                       (*1962*)

The Choir and Music of
Solitude and Silence

Silence is a great blue bell
Swinging and ringing, tinkling and singing,
In measure's pleasure, and in the supple symmetry
          of the soaring of the immense intense wings
          glinting against
All the blue radiance above us and within us, hidden
Save for the stars sparking, distant and unheard in their
          singing.
And this is the first meaning of the famous saying,
The stars sang. They are the white birds of silence
And the meaning of the difficult famous saying that the
          sons and daughters of morning sang,
Meant and means that they were and they are the children
          of God and morning,
Delighting in the lights of becoming and the houses of
          being,
Taking pleasure in measure and excess, in listening as in
          seeing.

Love is the most difficult and dangerous form of courage.
Courage is the most desperate, admirable and noble kind of
          love.

So that when the great blue bell of silence is stilled and
          stopped or broken
By the babel and chaos of desire unrequited, irritated and
          frustrated,
When the heart has opened and when the heart has spoken
Not of the purity and symmetry of gratification, but action
          of insatiable distraction's dissatisfaction,

Then the heart says, in all its blindness and faltering
    emptiness:
There is no God. Because I am hope. And hope must be
    fed.
And then the great blue bell of silence is deafened, dumbed,
    and has become the tomb of the living dead.

(*1959*)

News of the Gold World of May

News of the Gold World of May in Holland Michigan:

"Wooden shoes will clatter again
     on freshly scrubbed streets —"

The tulip will arise and reign again from awnings and
     windows
               of all colors and forms
               its vine, verve and valentine curves

               upon the city streets, the public grounds
                         and private lawns
               (wherever it is conceivable
               that a bulb might take root
                         and the two lips, softly curved, come up
               possessed by the skilled love and will of a
                    ballerina.)

The citizens will dance in folk dances.
               They will thump, they will pump,
               thudding and shoving
               elbow and thigh,
               bumping and laughing, like barrels and bells.

Vast fields of tulips in full bloom,
               the reproduction of a miniature Dutch village,
               part of a gigantic flower show.

                                        (1954?)

Occasional Poems

I *Christmas Poem for Nancy*

Noël, Noël
We live and we die
Between heaven and hell
Between the earth and the sky
And all shall be well
And all shall be unwell
And once again! all shall once again!
      All shall be well
By the ringing and the swinging
      of the great beautiful holiday bell
Of Noël! Noël!

(1958)

II *Salute Valentine*

I'll drink to thee only with my eyes
When two are three and four,
And guzzle reality's rise and cries
And praise the truth beyond surmise
When small shots shout: More! More! More! More!

(1961)

19

III *Rabbi to Preach*

Rabbi Robert Raaba will preach
    on "An Eye for an Eye"
        (an I for an I?)
(Two weeks from this week: "On the Sacred Would")
At Temple Sholem on Lake Shore Drive
— Pavel Slavensky will chant the liturgical responses
And William Leon, having now thirteen years
    will thank his parents that he exists
To celebrate his birthday of manhood, his chocolate
Bar Mitzvah, his yum-yum kippered herring, his Russian
    Corona.

                                  (*1959*)

The Greatest Thing in
North America

This is the greatest thing in North America:
Europe is the greatest thing in North America!
High in the sky, dark in the heart, and always there
Among the natural powers of sunlight and of air,
Changing, second by second, shifting and changing the
    light,
Bring fresh rain to the stone of the library steps.

Under the famous names upon the pediment:
        Thales, Aristotle,
Cicero, Augustine, Scotus, Galileo,
Joseph, Odysseus, Hamlet, Columbus and Spinoza,
Anna Karenina, Alyosha Karamazov, Sherlock Holmes.

And the last three also live upon the silver screen
Three blocks away, in moonlight's artificial day,
A double bill in the darkened palace whirled,
And the veritable glittering light of the turning world's
Burning mind and blazing imagination, showing, day by
    day
And week after week the desires of the heart and mind
Of all the living souls yearning everywhere
From Canada to Panama, from Brooklyn to Paraguay,
From Cuba to Vancouver, every afternoon and every night.

                                     (n.d.)

Metro-Goldwyn-Mayer

I looked toward the movie, the common dream,
The he and she in close-ups, nearer than life,
And I accepted such things as they seem,

The easy poise, the absence of the knife,
The near summer happily ever after,
The understood question, the immediate strife,

Not dangerous, nor mortal, but the fadeout
Enormously kissing amid warm laughter,
As if such things were not always played out

By an ignorant arm, which crosses the dark
And lights up a thin sheet with a shadow's mark.

(*1937*)

Love and Marilyn Monroe

(after Spillane)

Let us be aware of the true dark gods
Acknowledging the cache of the crotch
The primitive pure and powerful pink and grey
            private sensitivities
Wincing, marvelous in their sweetness, whence rises
            the future.

Therefore let us praise Miss Marilyn Monroe.
She has a noble attitude marked by pride and candor
She takes a noble pride in the female nature and torso
She articulates her pride with directness and exuberance
She is honest in her delight in womanhood and manhood.
She is not only a great lady, she is more than a lady,
She continues the tradition of Dolly Madison and Clara
  Bow
When she says, "Any woman who claims she does not like
            to be grabbed is a liar!"
Whether true or false, this colossal remark
            states a dazzling intention . . .

    It might be the birth of a new Venus among us
    It atones at the very least for such as Carrie Nation
    For Miss Monroe will never be a blue nose,
            and perhaps we may hope
    That there will be fewer blue noses because
            she has flourished —
    Long may she flourish in self-delight and the joy
            of womanhood.
    A nation haunted by Puritanism owes her homage and
            gratitude.

Let us praise, to say it again, her spiritual pride
And admire one who delights in what she has and is
(Who says also: "A woman is like a motor car:
       She needs a good body."
And: "I sun bathe in the nude, because I want
       to be blonde all over.")

    This is spiritual piety and physical ebullience
    This is the vivid glory, spiritual and physical,
    Of Miss Marilyn Monroe.

(1955?)

At This Moment of Time

Some who are uncertain compel me. They fear
The Ace of Spades. They fear
Love offered suddenly, turning from the mantelpiece,
Sweet with decision. And they distrust
The fireworks by the lakeside, first the spuft,
Then the colored lights, rising.
Tentative, hesitant, doubtful, they consume
Greedily Caesar at the prow returning
Locked in the stone of his act and office.
While the brass band brightly bursts over the water
They stand in the crowd lining the shore,
Aware of the water beneath Him. They know it. Their eyes
Are haunted by water.

Disturb me, compel me. If it is not true
"That no man is happy," that is not
The sense which guides you. If we are
Unfinished (we are, unless hope is a bad dream),
You are exact. What will come next
Has not yet come. You tug my sleeve
Before I speak, with a shadow's friendship,
And I remember that we who move
Are moved by clouds that darken midnight.

(1937)

25

Poem

You, my photographer, you, most aware,
Who climbed to the bridge when the iceberg struck,
Climbed with your camera when the ship's hull broke,
And lighted your flashes and, standing passionate there,
Wound the camera in the sudden burst's flare,
Shot the screaming women, and turned and took
Pictures of the iceberg (as the ship's deck shook)
Dreaming like the moon in the night's black air!

You, tiptoe on the rail to film a child!
The nude old woman swimming in the sea
Looked up from the dark water to watch you there;
Below, near the ballroom where the band still toiled,
The frightened, in their lifebelts, watched you bitterly —
You hypocrite! My brother! We are a pair!

(*1937*)

26

Poem

Old man in the crystal morning after snow,
Your throat swathed in a muffler, your bent
Figure building the snow man which is meant
For the grandchild's target,
                              do you know
This fat cartoon, his eyes pocked in with coal
Nears you each time your breath smokes the air,
Lewdly grinning out of a private nightmare?
He is the white cold shadow of your soul.

You build his comic head, you place his comic hat;
Old age is not so serious, and I
By the window sad and watchful as a cat,
Build to this poem of old age and of snow,
And weep: you are my snow man and I know
I near you, you near him, all of us must die.

(*1937*)

27

Spiders

Is the spider a monster in miniature?
His web is a cruel stair, to be sure,
Designed artfully, cunningly placed,
A delicate trap, carefully spun
To bind the fly (innocent or unaware)
In a net as strong as a chain or a gun.

There are far more spiders than the man in the street
    supposes
And the philosopher-king imagines, let alone knows!
There are six hundred kinds of spiders and each one
Differs in kind and in unkindness.
In variety of behavior spiders are unrivalled:
The fat garden spider sits motionless, amidst or at the heart
Of the orb of its web: other kinds run,
Scuttling across the floor, falling into bathtubs,
Trapped in the path of its own wrath, by overconfidence
    drowned and undone.

Other kinds — more and more kinds under the stars and
    the sun —
Are carnivores: all are relentless, ruthless
Enemies of insects. Their methods of getting food
Are unconventional, numerous, various and sometimes
    hilarious:
Some spiders spin webs as beautiful
As Japanese drawings, intricate as clocks, strong as rocks:
Others construct traps which consist only
Of two sticky and tricky threads. Yet this ambush is
    enough

To bind and chain a crawling ant for long enough:
The famished spider feels the vibration
Which transforms patience into sensation and satiation.
The handsome wolf spider moves suddenly freely and relies
Upon lightning suddenness, stealth and surprise,
Possessing accurate eyes, pouncing upon his victim with
    the speed of surmise.

Courtship is dangerous: there are just as many elaborate
    and endless techniques and varieties
As characterize the wooing of more analytic, more
    introspective beings: Sometimes the male
Arrives with the gift of a freshly caught fly.
Sometimes he ties down the female, when she is frail,
With deft strokes and quick maneuvres and threads of silk:
But courtship and wooing, whatever their form, are
    informed
By extreme caution, prudence, and calculation,
For the female spider, lazier and fiercer than the male
    suitor,
May make a meal of him if she does not feel in the same
    mood, or if her appetite
Consumes her far more than the revelation of love's
    consummation.
Here among spiders, as in the higher forms of nature,
The male runs a terrifying risk when he goes seeking for
    the bounty of beautiful Alma Magna Mater:
Yet clearly and truly he must seek and find his mate and
    match like every other living creature!

(1959)

To Helen

(After Valéry)

O Sea! . . . 'Tis I, risen from death once more
To hear the waves' harmonious roar
And see the galleys, sharp, in dawn's great awe
Raised from the dark by the rising and gold oar.

My fickle hands sufficed to summon kings
Their salt beards amused my fingers, deft and pure.
I wept. They sang of triumphs now obscure:
And the first abyss flooded the hull as if with falling wings.

I hear the profound horns and trumpets of war
Matching the rhythm, swinging of the flying oars:
The galleys' chant enchains the foam of sound;
And the gods, exalted at the heroic prow,
E'en though the spit of spray insults each smiling brow,
Beckon to me, with arms indulgent, frozen, sculptured,
            and dead long long ago.

(*1962*)

30

From *The Graveyard by the Sea*

(After Valéry)

This hushed surface where the doves parade
Amid the pines vibrates, amid the graves;
Here the noon's justice unites all fires when
The sea aspires forever to begin again and again.
O what a gratification comes after long meditation
O satisfaction, after long meditation or ratiocination
Upon the calm of the gods
Upon divine serenity, in luxurious contemplation!

What pure toil of perfect lightning enwombs, consumes,
Each various manifold jewel of imperceptible foam,
And how profound a peace appears to be begotten and
    begun
When upon the abyss the sunlight seems to pause,
The pure effects of an eternal cause:
Time itself sparkles, to dream and to know are one. . . .

(*1961*)

The Spring

(After Rilke)

Spring has returned! Everything has returned!
The earth, just like a schoolgirl, memorizes
Poems, so many poems. . . . Look, she has learned
So many famous poems, she has earned so many prizes!

Teacher was strict. We delighted in the white
Of the old man's beard, bright like the snow's:
Now we may ask which names are wrong, or right
For "blue," for "apple," for "ripe." She knows, she knows!

Lucky earth, let out of school, now you must play
Hide-and-seek with all the children every day:
You must hide that we may seek you: we will! We will!

The happiest child will hold you. She knows all the things
You taught her: the word for "hope," and for "believe,"
Are still upon her tongue. She sings and sings and sings.

(1965)

Late Autumn in Venice

(After Rilke)

The city floats no longer like a bait
To hook the nimble darting summer days.
The glazed and brittle palaces pulsate and radiate
And glitter. Summer's garden sways,
A heap of marionettes hanging down and dangled,
Leaves tired, torn, turned upside down and strangled:
Until from forest depths, from bony leafless trees
A will wakens: the admiral, lolling long at ease,
Has been commanded, overnight — suddenly —:
In the first dawn, all galleys put to sea!
Waking then in autumn chill, amid the harbor medley,
The fragrance of pitch, pennants aloft, the butt
Of oars, all sails unfurled, the fleet
Awaits the great wind, radiant and deadly.

(*1965*)

33

Archaic Bust of Apollo

(After Rilke)

We cannot know the indescribable face
Where the eyes like apples ripened. Even so,
His torso has a candelabra's glow,
His gaze, contained as in a mirror's grace,

Shines within it. Otherwise his breast
Would not be dazzling. Nor would you recognize
The smile that moves along his curving thighs,
There where love's strength is caught within its nest.

This stone would not be broken, but intact
Beneath the shoulders' flowing cataract,
Nor would it glisten like a stallion's hide,

Brimming with radiance from every side
As a star sparkles. Now it is dawn once more.
All places scrutinize you. You must be reborn.

(1965)

II

What a Poem Knows

The Journey of a Poem Compared to All the Sad Variety of Travel

A poem moves forward,
    Like the passages and percussions of trains in progress
    A pattern of recurrence, a hammer of repetetive
        occurrence

    a slow less and less heard
    low thunder under all passengers

Steel sounds tripping and tripled and
Grinding, revolving, gripping, turning, and returning
as the flung carpet of the wide countryside spreads out on
        each side in billows

And in isolation, rolled out, white house, red barn, squat
    silo,
Pasture, hill, meadow and woodland pasture
And the striped poles step fast past the train windows
Second after second takes snapshots, clicking,
Into the dangled boxes of glinting windows
Snapshots and selections, rejections, at angles, of shadows
A small town: a shop's sign — GARAGE; and then white
    gates
Where waiting cars wait with the unrest of trembling
Breathing hard and idling, until the slow descent
Of the red cones of sunset: a dead march: a slow tread and
    heavy

Of the slowed horses of Apollo
— Until the slowed horses of Apollo go over the horizon
And all things are parked, slowly or willingly,
into the customary or at random places.   (*1962*)

Philology Recapitulates Ontology, Poetry Is Ontology

Faithful to your commandments, o consciousness, o

Holy bird of words soaring ever whether to nothingness or
      to inconceivable fulfillment slowly:

And still I follow you, awkward as that dandy of ontology
      and as awkward as his albatross and as

another dandy of ontology before him, another shepherd
      and watchdog of being, the one who

Talked forever of forever as if forever of having been
      and being an ancient mariner,

Hesitant forever as if forever were the albatross

Hung round his neck by the seven seas of the seven muses,

and with as little conclusion, since being never concludes,

Studying the sibilance and the splashing of the seas and of
      seeing and of being's infinite seas,

Staring at the ever-blue and the far small stars and
      the faint white endless curtain of the
      twinkling play's endless seasons.

(1959)

Poem

Faithful to your commands, o consciousness, o

Beating wings, I studied

the roses and the muses of reality,

the deceptions and the deceptive elation of the redness of
the growing morning,

and all the greened and thorned variety of the vines of
error, which begin by promising

Everything and more than everything, and then suddenly,

At the height of noon seem to rise to the peak or dune-like
moon of no return

So that everything is or seems to have become nothing, or
of no genuine importance:

And it is not that the departure of hope or its sleep has
made it inconceivable

That anything should be or should have been important:

It is the belief that hope itself was not, from the beginning,
before believing, the most important of all beliefs.

(*1962*)

What Curious Dresses All Men Wear

What curious dresses all men wear!
The walker you met in a brown study,
The President smug in rotogravure,
The mannequin, the bathing beauty.

The bubble-dancer, the deep-sea diver,
The bureaucrat, the adulterer,
Hide private parts which I disclose
To those who know what a poem knows.

(*1938?*)

Sonnet Suggested by Homer, Chaucer, Shakespeare, Edgar Allan Poe, Paul Valéry, James Joyce, et al.

Let me not, ever, to the marriage in Cana
Of Galilee admit the slightest sentiment
Of doubt about the astonishing and sustaining manna
Of chance and choice to throw a shadow's element
Of disbelief in truth — Love is not love
Nor is the love of love its truth in consciousness
If it can be made hesitant by any crow or dove or
       seeming angel or demon from above or from below
Or made more than it is knows itself to be by the authority
       of any ministry of love.

O no — it is the choice of chances and the chancing of
       all choice — the wine
which was the water may be sickening, unsatisfying or
       sour
A new barbiturate drawn from the fattest flower
That prospers green on Lethe's shore. For every hour
Denies or once again affirms the vow and the ultimate
       tower
Of aspiration which made Ulysses toil so far away from
       home
And then, for years, strive against every wanton desire,
       sea and fire, to return across the
       ever-threatening seas
A journey forever far beyond all the vivid eloquence
       of every poet and all poetry.

(*1964*)

41

Sonnet on Famous and Familiar Sonnets and Experiences

(With much help from Robert Good, William Shakespeare, John Milton, and little Catherine Schwartz)

Shall I compare her to a summer play?
She is too clever, too devious, too subtle, too dark:
Her lies are rare, but then she paves the way
Beyond the summer's sway, within the jejune park
Where all souls' aspiration to true nobility
Obliges Statues in the Frieze of Death
And when this pantomime and Panama of Panorama Fails,
"I'll never speak to you agayne" — or waste her panting
    breath.

When I but think of how her years are spent
Deadening that one talent which — for woman is —
Death or paralysis, denied: nature's intent
That each girl be a mother — whether or not she is
Or has become a lawful wife or bride
— O Alma Magna Mater, deathless the living death of
    pride.

(*1961*)

Yeats Died Saturday in France

Yeats died Saturday in France.
Freedom from his animal
Has come at last in alien Nice,
His heart beat separate from his will:
He knows at last the old abyss
Which always faced his staring face.

No ability, no dignity
Can fail him now who trained so long
For the outrage of eternity,
Teaching his heart to beat a song
In which man's strict humanity,
Erect as a soldier, became a tongue.

(*1939*)

From: *A King of Kings,*
A King among the Kings

Come, let us rejoice in James Joyce, in the greatness of this
   poet,
         king, and king of poets

For he is our poor dead king, he is the monarch and Caesar
   of English,
         he is the veritable King of the King's English

               The English of the life of the city,
               and the English of music;

Let them rejoice because he rejoiced and was joyous;

For his joy was superior, it was supreme, for it was
   accomplished

After the suffering of much evil, the evil of the torment of
   pride,

By the overcoming of disgust and despair by means of the
   confrontation
         of them

By the enduring of nausea, the supporting of exile, the
   drawing from
               the silence of exile, the pure arias of the
               hidden music of all things, all beings.

For the joy of Joyce was earned by the sweat of the bow of
   his mind

by the tears of the agony of his heart;

hence it was gained, mastered, and
  conquered,
    (hence it was not a gift and freely
      given,
    a mercy often granted to masters,
    as if they miraculous were natural —)

For he earned his joy and ours by the domination of evil by
              confrontation and the exorcism of
                language
              in all its powers of imitation and
              imagination and radiance and
                delight. . . .

                                        (*n.d.*)

Now He Knows All There Is to Know: Now He Is Acquainted With the Day and Night

(Robert Frost, 1875–1963)

Whose wood this is I think I know:
He made it sacred long ago:
He will expect me, far or near
To watch that wood immense with snow.

That famous horse must feel great fear
Now that his noble rider's no longer here:
He gives his harness bells to rhyme
— Perhaps he will be back, in time?

All woulds were promises he kept
Throughout the night when others slept:
Now that he knows all that he did not know,
His wood is holy, and full of snow,
and all the beauty he made holy long long ago
In Boston, London, Washington,
And once by the Pacific and once in Moscow:
> *and now, and now*
> *upon the fabulous blue river ever*
> *or singing from a great white bough*

And wherever America is, now as before,
> and now as long, long ago
He sleeps and wakes forever more!

> *"O what a metaphysical victory*
> *The first day and night of death must be!"*

(1963)

46

A Dream of Whitman Paraphrased, Recognized and Made More Vivid by Renoir

Twenty-eight naked young women bathed by the shore
Or near the bank of a woodland lake
Twenty-eight girls and all of them comely
Worthy of Mack Sennett's camera and Florenz Ziegfield's
  Foolish Follies.

They splashed and swam with the wondrous
  unconsciousness
Of their youth and beauty
In the full spontaneity and summer of the fleshes of
  awareness
Heightened, intensified and softened
By the soft and the silk of the waters
Blooded made ready by the energy set afire by the
  nakedness of the body,

Electrified: deified: undenied.

A young man of thirty years beholds them from a distance.
He lives in the dungeon of ten million dollars.
He is rich, handsome and empty standing behind the linen
  curtains
Beholding them.
Which girl does he think most desirable, most beautiful?
They are all equally beautiful and desirable from the gold
  distance.
For if poverty darkens discrimination and makes
  perception too vivid,
The gold of wealth is also a form of blindness.
For has not a Frenchman said, Although this is America . . .

What he has said is not entirely relevant,
That a naked woman is a proof of the existence of God.

Where is he going?
Is he going to be among them to splash and to laugh with
    them?
They did not see him although he saw them and was there
    among them.
He saw them as he would not have seen them had they
    been conscious
Of him or conscious of men in complete depravation:
This is his enchantment and impoverishment
As he possesses them in gaze only.

. . . He felt the wood secrecy, he knew the June softness
The warmth surrounding him crackled
        Held in by the mansard roof mansion
He glimpsed the shadowy light on last year's brittle leaves
    fallen,
        Looked over and overlooked, glimpsed by the fall
            of death,
Winter's mourning and the May's renewal.

                                                    (1962)

Albert Einstein to
Archibald MacLeish

I should have been a plumber fixing drains
And mending pure white bathtubs for the great Diogenes
(who scorned all lies, all liars, and all tyrannies),

And then, perhaps, he would bestow on me — majesty!
(O modesty aside, forgive my fallen pride, O hidden
    majesty,
The lamp, the lantern, the lucid light he sought for
        All too often — sick humanity!)

(*1961*)

The Poet

The riches of the poet are equal to his poetry
His power is his left hand
        It is idle weak and precious
His poverty is his wealth, a wealth which may destroy him
    like Midas
Because it is that laziness which is a form of impatience
And this he may be destroyed by the gold of the light
    which never was
On land or sea.
He may be drunken to death, draining the casks of excess
That extreme form of success.
He may suffer Narcissus' destiny
Unable to live except with the image which is infatuation
Love, blind, adoring, overflowing
Unable to respond to anything which does not bring love
    quickly or immediately.

. . . The poet must be innocent and ignorant
But he cannot be innocent since stupidity is not his strong
    point
Therefore Cocteau said, "What would I not give
To have the poems of my youth withdrawn from
    existence?
I would give to Satan my immortal soul."
This metaphor is wrong, for it is his immortal soul which
    he wished to redeem,
Lifting it and sifting it, free and white, from the actuality of
        youth's banality, vulgarity,
        pomp and affectation of his early
        works of poetry.

So too in the same way a Famous American Poet
When fame at last had come to him sought out the fifty
   copies
of his first book of poems which had been privately printed
by himself at his own expense.
He succeeded in securing 48 of the 50 copies, burned them
And learned then how the last copies were extant,
As the law of the land required, stashed away in the
   national capital,
at the Library of Congress.
Therefore he went to Washington, therefore he took out
   the last two copies
Placed them in his pocket, planned to depart
Only to be halted and apprehended. Since he was the
   author,
Since they were his books and his property he was
   reproached
But forgiven. But the two copies were taken away from him
Thus setting a national precedent.

For neither amnesty nor forgiveness is bestowed upon
   poets, poetry and poems,
For William James, the lovable genius of Harvard
spoke the terrifying truth: *"Your friends may forget, God
       may forgive you, But the brain cells record
       your acts for the rest of eternity."*
What a terrifying thing to say!
This is the endless doom, without remedy, of poetry.
This is also the joy everlasting of poetry.

(1954)

Apollo Musagete, Poetry, and the Leader of the Muses

Nothing is given which is not taken.

Little or nothing is taken which is not freely desired,
   freely, truly and fully.

"You would not seek me if you had not found me": this is
   true of all that is supremely desired and admired . . .

"An enigma is an animal," said the hurried, harried
   schoolboy:

And a horse divided against itself cannot stand;

And a moron is a man who believes in having too many
   wives: what harm is there in that?

O the endless fecundity of poetry is equaled
By its endless inexhaustible freshness, as in the discovery
   of America and of poetry.

Hence it is clear that the truth is not strait and narrow but
   infinite:
All roads lead to Rome and to poetry
      and to poem, sweet poem
      and from, away and towards are the same typography.

Hence the poet must be, in a way, stupid and naive and a
   little child;

Unless ye be as a little child ye cannot enter the kingdom
    of poetry.

Hence the poet must be able to become a tiger like Blake; a
    carousel like Rilke.

Hence he must be all things to be free, for all
    impersonations
        a doormat and a monument
        to all situations possible or actual
The cuckold, the cuckoo, the conqueror, and the coxcomb.

It is to him in the zoo that the zoo cries out and the hyena:
"Hello, take off your hat, king of the beasts, and be seated,
    Mr. Bones."

And hence the poet must seek to be essentially
    anonymous.
    He must die a little death each morning.
        He must swallow his toad and study his vomit
            as Baudelaire studied *la charogne* of Jeanne
            Duval.

The poet must be or become both Keats and Renoir and
    Keats *as* Renoir.
Mozart as Figaro and Edgar Allan Poe as Ophelia, stoned
    out of her mind
        drowning in the river called forever river and
        ever . . .

Keats as Mimi, Camille, and an aging gourmet.
He must also refuse the favors of the unattainable lady
(As Baudelaire refused Madame Sabatier when the fair
    blonde summoned him,

For Jeanne Duval was enough and more than enough,
    although she cuckolded him
With errand boys, servants, waiters; reality was Jeanne
    Duval.
Had he permitted Madame Sabatier to teach the poet a
    greater whiteness,
His devotion and conception of the divinity of Beauty
    would have suffered an absolute diminution.)

The poet must be both Casanova and St. Anthony,

He must be Adonis, Nero, Hippolytus, Heathcliff, and
    Phaedre,
        Genghis Kahn, Genghis Cohen, and Gordon
        Martini
            Dandy Ghandi and St. Francis,

Professor Tenure, and Dizzy the dean and Disraeli of
    Death.

He would have worn the horns of existence upon his head,
He would have perceived them regarding the looking-glass,
He would have needed them the way a moose needs a
    hatrack;
Above his heavy head and in his loaded eyes, black and
    scorched,
He would have seen the meaning of the hat-rack, above the
    glass
Looking in the dark foyer.

For the poet must become nothing but poetry,
He must be nothing but a poem when he is writing
Until he is absent-minded as the dead are
        Forgetful as the nymphs of Lethe and a
        lobotomy . . .
            ("the fat weed that rots on Lethe wharf").

He must be Iago, Desdemona, and a willow tree;
He must be torn between church and state . . . like
    Antigone
            (father and life . . .)

He must be a nymphomaniacal whore yet preserve his
    virginity,
The virginity of the empty paper's whiteness, snow and
    liberty;
Unless he succeeds, how can he unite in a single thought
          Morning and death
          (Desire and transcendence)?

          How can he possess
        The dreams and extremes of hope and despair
          (which are named Death and morning)?

He must wish to dance at everyone's wedding.
He must wish to be everyone and everything,
He must be a Trappist, but eloquent as Trotsky,

          Chaste but a gigolo,
          The Czar yet Figaro.

Hence, how can he be anything but nothing or zero

If this dramatis persona is ever a necessity?

                      (1962)

III

The Studies of Narcissus

Prologue

Narcissus, speaking in the first person — or at times in the third person (in retrospect) — describes his passion and the various forms of misunderstanding which others have committed, regarding his behavior. Others — all the others, including the nymph, Echo — thought Narcissus was moved by self-love and looked in the river only to see his own beloved face. They forgot that his father was the river god; and they misinterpreted the devotion and concentration, excluding all other things, with which he gazed upon the river's surface as a love of his own which rejected the offered and eager love of all the others, remaining unaware of the meaning of his gaze upon the river at night or when the sky was so clouded over that he could not see his own face. Echo, like all the others, believed that he had fallen in love with himself so much that, being in love with him and misconceiving the nature of love, she imitated his voice and his very words, thinking that this was what he desired and what would make her desirable. The truth was that he was entirely dissatisfied with the image of his own face, yet the river, continuously changing under the continuously changing light, and promising so much to Narcissus, nurtured an inexhaustible hope in him, and hopes: the hope that he would be satisfied, and beautiful enough, as an image, a face and a being, to be able to be loved by a truly beautiful being. But the river itself was the most beautiful of all the beings he had ever beheld.

Overture

The mind is a city like London,
Smoky and populous: it is a capital
Like Rome, ruined and eternal,
Marked by the monuments which no one
Now remembers. For the mind, like Rome, contains
Catacombs, aqueducts, amphitheatres, palaces,
Churches and equestrian statues, fallen, broken or soiled.
The mind possesses and is possessed by all the ruins
Of every haunted, hunted generation's celebration.

"Call us what you will: we are made such by love."
We are such studs as dreams are made on, and
Our little lives are ruled by the gods, by Pan,
Piping of all, seeking to grasp or grasping
All of the grapes; and by the bow-and-arrow god,
Cupid, piercing the heart through, suddenly and forever.

Dusk we are, to dusk returning, after the burning,
After the gold fall, the fallen ash, the bronze,
Scattered and rotten, after the white null statues which
Are winter, sleep, and nothingness: when
Will the houselights of the universe
Light up and blaze?
                    For it is not the sea
Which murmurs in a shell,
And it is not only heart, at harp o'clock,
It is the dread terror of the uncontrollable
Horses of the apocalypse, running in wild dread
toward Arcturus — and returning as suddenly. . . .

Alone, obsessed as the devout, I waited:
Under the mast of my head, my eyes sailed forth,
Fed by an abundance so multitudinous
I knew it must be infinite:
Between the sleek, rippling and glittering silks
Delight in the light mounted and mounted in me
                    and doubt itself
                    and doubt
Fathered the dolls of possibility
Until they shone as the progeny of hope,
The dazzling diamonds my demon denied and loved
— Distant or hidden sources nurtured the sorcery
And miracles of radiance, flowed out of depths
Or struck, like lightning, from heights I merely guessed.

How the sky shone: look how my leaves are curved
And black, how they possess and are possessed
By every brilliance, radiance, and vividness —
— How could they know I had discovered the self?
By studying the marvels of my hope
And all the variety and poverty of my face
Within the supple marble where the leaves
Of swirling waters were more numerous,
                    as various
As falsehood, more fecund than fantasy,
And infinite as numbers . . . space was a colosseum,
And infinite as numbers . . .
The silence was the drum, and drums, of space,
Waiting and beating,
Throbbing, expectant, before all triumph, all miracles
            to come. . . .

Within the river's folds and folding fields
I gazed until I looked for the rippled dream

Of seeing myself at last a being I loved,
Loved by a being beautiful enough to love —

. . . The river holds the summer's pride, the sum
Of sun and summer, gold and golding glow:
Love is reality — as in the beginning it was —
And love is destiny. The reality of the ecstasy
Riding into the womb begot the city,
Planted or sowed the future's flowers and powers
        . . . again, again . . .
Inmost was utmost:
Under the mast of my head
My eyes sailed forth and searched
The sleek silks and curving softnesses:
The river was reality and various plurality
And made me other than I was at each
Ripple of its irresistible flowing:
I thought: God is in love, in love with possibility,
His love are his loves, his love is enough
To make the promiscuity of actuality . . .
— The river was full of bells as the sun rose,
Shuddering ripples grew to the radiance
Of chandeliers at noon, the blazing sun
Became a jewel of inexhaustible opulence. . . .

The blazing sunlight is the world itself:
The black heart of the ego shines and shines in vain,
Weak as the moonlight, like a kind of moonlight —

The river rose from sovereign sources, secret steeps,
Until, under the sun, it was a dream of diamonds

Or in the winter, frozen, within
The snow's hushed infinite,
It was a kind of moonlight,
A pathos of white silence, white
And silent, lighted by the moon's white silence —

How blond the light of summer is, how round
And how profound the blue contained and loved
Within the river's flowing glass, glinting and glittering —
Brightening and darkening, freshening, shadowing
In its irresistible going and going, holding
Glowing, and glowing being's immense plurality!

The game of the mystery of reality
Began when the first thought concealed itself,
When the speech of ripened lips
Hid what was already hidden, or not yet known.

For long as lore, desire was narrative,
Gratified in imagination's will,
And longer still I read the handsome story —
Venus as absolute in joy's full glory!

Eternity is the roar you hear
When you hold a sea shell close to your ear.

It is not the sound of the knock of the pounding heart,
It is not the roar of the insatiable sea, erupting upon the
    shore,

It is the eternal roar of eternity, the lightning and the
    thunder
Of each moment's subjection and rejection — the eternal
            roar of judgment and resurrection —

... After utter forgiveness, what knowledge
Can be possessed by consciousness?
Forgive: do not forget. Remember and live,
For life is rooted in memory's damnation and blessedness.
And life is hope, hope rooted in the past as it is
            known, remembered, and controlled
            by the future's hopes, the future's flowers.

Look: I looked at the dancers, swaying,
Under the lanterns, in the olive garden,
            the fat vineyard, the apple orchard,
Or bordering the river where the boats are anchored,
Bound to the shore and lolling, like the dancers:
They do not know the secret of summer,
They do not possess the natural knowledge of the river,
Yet they sigh and quicken, murmur to the music,
Delighted that they exist, for all love's agony
            and all love's ecstasy,
They are not ashamed they touch each other, nor afraid
They are beautiful enough to touch and love,
They wish to touch each other, touching and touched,
Before the cause becomes the truth, before the root
            Becomes the fruit, because. . . .

We are all — look! — the figments of the imagination's
    aspiration!
Are the follies or followers of intense and hot infatuation:

Each heart is liege to Venus, queen and empress of the
        seas and ports of consciousness;
And thus, as Venus from the sea arose and came to be,
The self I know, Narcissus as he is known, was born,
        within the river, arising shocked —
Gazing or gaping at the river's ever-being, ever-becoming:
The river was my mother: it was my school
And was and is the only school because
Knowledge is only the knowledge of love,
And every story is the story of love,
And every storyteller is a lovelorn ghost!

The river was the abundant belly of beauty itself,
The river was the dream space where I walked,
The river was itself and yet it was — flowing and
    freshening —
A self anew, another self, or self renewed
At every tick of eternity, and by each glint of light
Mounting or sparkling, descending to shade and black
— Had I but told them my heart, told how it was
Taunted at noon and pacified at dusk, at starfall midnight
Strong in hope once more, ever in eagerness
Jumping like joy, would they have heard? How could they?
How, when what they knew was, like the grass,
Simple and certain, known through the truth of touch,
        another form and fountain of falsehood's fecundity —
Gazing upon their faces as they gazed
Could they have seen my faces as whores who are
Holy and deified as priestesses of hope
        — the sacred virgins of futurity —
Promising dear divinity precisely because
They were disfigured ducks who might become
And be, and ever beloved, white swans, noble and
    beautiful.
            Could they have seen how my faces were

Bonfires of worship and vigil, blazes of adoration
                and hope
— Surely they would have laughed again, renewed their
    scorn,
Giggled and snickered, cruel. Surely have said
This is the puerile mania of the obsessed,
The living logic of the lunatic:
I was the statue of their merriment,
Dead and a death, Pharaoh and monster forsaken and lost.

My faces were my apes: my apes became
Performers in the Sundays of their parks,
Buffoons or clowns in the comedy or farce
When they took pleasure in knowing that they were not
    like me.

I waited like obsession in solitude:
The sun's white terror tore and roared at me,
The moonlight, almond white, at night,
Whether awake or sleeping, arrested me
And sang, softly, haunted, unlike the sun
But as the sun. Withheld from me or took away
Despair or peace, making me once more
With thought of what had never been before —
— The others were the despots of despair —

The river's freshness sailed from unknown sources —

. . . They snickered giggled, laughed aloud at last,
They mocked and marvelled at the statue which was

A caricature, as strained and stiff, and yet
A statue of self-love! — since self-love was
To them, truly my true love, how, then, was I a stillness of
   nervousness
So nervous a caricature: did they suppose
Self-love was unrequited, or betrayed?
They thought I had fallen in love with my own face,
And this belief became the night-like obstacle
To understanding all my unbroken suffering,
My studious soft-regard, the pain of hope,
The torment of possibility:
How then could I have expected them to see me
As I saw myself, within my gaze, or see
That being thus seemed as a toad, a frog, a wen, a mole.
Knowing their certainty that I was only
A monument, a monster who had fallen in love
With himself alone, how could I have
Told them what was in me, within my heart, trembling,
   and passionate
Within the labyrinth and caves of my mind, which is
Like every mind partly or wholly hidden from itself?
The words for what is in my heart and in my mind
Do not exist: But I must seek and search to find
Amid the vines and orchards of the vivid world of day
Approximate images, imaginary parallels
For what is in my heart and dark within my mind:
Comparisons and mere metaphors: for all
Of them are substitutes, both counterfeit and vague:
They are, at most, deceptive resemblances,
False in their very likeness, like the sons
Who are alike and kin and more unlike and false
Because they seem the father's very self: but each one is
— Although begotten by the same forbears — himself,
The unique self, each one is unique, like every other one,
And everything, older or younger, nevertheless
A passionate nonesuch who before has been.

Do you hear, do you see? Do you understand me now, and
   how
The words for what is my heart do not exist?

Once, far from me in the distance, in a grove, concealed
Hidden, she thought, I heard a girl
Screaming with joy, joy absolute,
Joy unheard of before, and never known,
And given to me or given
By me to girls: I had never been. . . .
How many thoughts, like lightning strokes, occurred
And seemed more true than any truth I knew!

Came with no concentration, no
Concern or effort, toiling up the path,
Sparkled like the radiance or stood like the oars
Whence all the radiance arrives, the sunlight's swords:

Each thought an intuition, instant,
Spontaneous, coherent in the mind
Of words: and seemed and were and are
— As first I named them — endless sentences
Proven abundantly in all the instances
Experience unveiled, although it was
— In so many other ways — astonishing!

This was an endless sentence which I learned
Or recognized in the fluent river's school:
Everything is always somewhere else; or it is

Present — when undesired — in an embarrassment
Of riches, a profusion prolific and inexhaustible,
An oppression of luxury, like Midas's gold.

This is an endless sentence which I saw
As student at the river's universal school:
The cause of that boundless ecstasy in which
A man had plunged that screaming girl,
— A triumph so triumphant all is lost
Save for the sweetness at the source
Within, intense, of such an intensity
That blessed in the loss of consciousness
It seems, at first, a kind of death — so much
Like death that the fearful self, beholds beholding
Upon the brink, all of the terror of love,
Draws back and the first time never is endured!

I knew the parable of trying to see
The truth behind the face, the mind behind
The surface, the radiance within
The radiance, within the shining radiance
And thus I missed matchless magnificence
So many times! Since, at times,
Appearance is reality and not a mask —
        neither secret nor masked:
The apple is the apple which is red
And ripe upon the tree — but only then
During the time of ripening, before
The fall, long long after the flower
— The times of flowering and the flowers are
The scenes of falsehood most of all!

This too is a parable of reality,
It is as well a parable of love,
And love's reality, after the flowers,
After the green and growing fruit.

I was, for a long time, every kind
Of shining angel: kind of angle,
And kind of light: each point of view
Drew up something new, or some which
I never knew. Every picture possessed
Four sides, and four thousand sides and sights.
Each time I looked or read between the lines
I saw the mount of Venus suddenly.
I found myself upon the island named
Cytherea — the lake of summer capital.

I visited the house of Orpheus,
His house, his garden and his park,
The horses which he loved and which he lost . . .
Finding the beasts of hell, to whom he sang
Not to regain his lost Eurydice,
But to be free of the ice-like pain and stone of loss.
— The music which he made and sang to gain
That liberty was strange, a strangeness and a mockery.

The present is the future. We are there
— Or going where we wished to be — the past
Is but a version of the future which
Is likely to be false. The present is
The future twice: first it is the future of the hope
By which we live and die, direct or drive the will

Of toil, the mind of effort; second, it is
The comparison of the present as it is
And as it was conceived by hope, before,
When past was present still, not yet unmasked.

How many structures of reality
I saw within the river: light which was at once
Insight, the sweet access of being which
The radiance of knowledge gives and gives
With a purity and freedom which no other thing,
Consumed, confers, neither the bread nor wine
On which we fed on the dark god's holidays.

                                    Height:
                                    Light:
The river of all rivers, the motion of emotion
The feeling of the real and [*words missing*]
The feast of reality and
Your holy word
An infinite bliss, given as
Infinitely as
It is infinitely gifted:
Let it be, let your kingdom
Descend in all splendor
When we ring
The bells of morning and the bells of mortality
Swinging and singing
                    as the ever freshness
Which flowers forever in the dark patience
Of the strength of hope and the truth
Of the heart which the heart itself
Seldom knows, and never wholly believes.

You would not have found
What is so precious to you, if you had not
Been seeking it. And: if you had sought it,
You would not have found it: Let it come! Let it come!

This is true too: if you find only
What you bring in your seeking,
— Yet: you would not have found it,
If you had not been able to recognize it!

— This is the dynasty of discovery:
It is ruled by a dialectic of poles apart:
                    The synthesis is thus:

It is true. It is not real:
You find what you possess: you seek
What you do not know you have
                    that you possess.

The river sang: there are many truths,
Look: how they glitter and ripple, radiant,
And the river chanted: many truths — did you know?
                    do you believe?
Are better than one truth. This is
The doctrine of the magician and musician:
But reality is magical and musical.
It comprehends the stones and the hearts of men.
And all the variety between these two
Extremes completes the comparison
Which makes all dreams poor and inadequate
Once set in contrast with reality's ingenuity.

Those who knew passion and compassion after me
Misunderstood my purity, my poverty,
The elation through privation, the motion of devotion.

Sisyphus, Oedipus, Theseus, Heracles,
Cupid and Psyche . . .

      They never knew — or knew for the first time,
      The [*word missing*] of the rain,
             nor for the first time
Knew the new flow of the heartbeats of love,
A thing — and experience — which, never having been
              known before
Did not possess the status of what exists,
          the dusk of doubt,
But merely the status of hope, the state of dusk
And doubt,and fear, rising and falling.

. . . It is not true: it never has been true.
The moon shines on the loved and the unloved
The music mounted to the minds
Of those who could and those who could not hear:
The music blooming, blossoming, flowering and flowing
   forth
For those who have fallen or are falling in love:
Behold it — behold that ghost of sentiment —
       that ghostly
           and sentimental ghost.

At first the river was a simple window
Empty, in shadow: immensity was a waste:

How wide the silence was, when I looked up
Beholding the sky's blue capital,
Thinking it empty, although beautiful
. . . I did not think it was the louver of the dead,
Nor think it was the palace of the stars' dancers —

— How could they understand my study and my hope
Or understand the study of hope itself
When all the knowledge came, at last, to this?
That all hope is at heart only then hope
That hope is true, or at least true enough,
That hope itself will still be possible
After each new illusion and conclusion,
And after each recognition of delusion!

Since love is reality, reality is love!
And the fear of the fading of feeling
Is the disease of the withering of hope, the hope
That the self will, at last, be born again anew, renewed
— Will wholly arise
When the living awaken
From the thickets of sleep and the mines of night,
Withdrawing from the death of self-deception,
No longer master nor monster, no longer
Demon nor despot, strong, strong as illusion, stronger . . .

What blooms after the lisping, lipping dimnesses
When night in all its formless vagueness is over all
The beauty of the body of the river?
The roses are pink because of the weight of fragrance.
The leaves are green because green aspires to arise to
    radiance.

The river is the ripening or the ripened
Harvest of all the passing shows which move and shine
Between the soil, the sun, and the brilliant or dark sky.

The river is the hymn wherein
The ultimate vineyards of variety
Become the plums and grapes of dawn and dusk
In a plenitude so multitudinous
It must be infinite and infinitely generous:
It is the dance in which abundance falls and follows,
          forever moving
In all the moods and modes of fertility and fruitfulness.
— Branches, trees, brooded over the pool:
Salmon slipped lithely under the ripples, in grooves
And the salmon of the sunlight still gleamed until
All became [*manuscript breaks off*]. . . .

O the brio, & presto, & allegro of the river when
               the sun
Blazed down on it, and it sang, mingling brights and
               blues:
What ghost a sovereign ruled the sources, distant,
               concealed,
Changing the depths under the merrying light, mica-
     glittering
               so furious: so joyous:
                    so spontaneous!

A suave bush.

I was in the presence of the mystery
Of the amplitude of abundance, dancing,

Multitudinous abundance, the majesty
Of ample infinitude, flowing and overflowing.

I was in the presence of the mystery
Of the plenitude and the majesty
Of the gifts and the giving and the grant
Of the ever-flowing process of reality:
Love is knowing in unknowing
Love is the majesty of the mystery
Of the abundance of surrender
When suddenly all the senses chant,
And the mind, caught in the anthem,
[*missing lines*]

Who but the fallen angel of consciousness
Sings with so much radiance of the clarity of reality?
The mastery of victory? The reality of hope?

I have supped and sucked and sickened in the valley
          of desperation.
I have been terrified — and in the darkness lost,
I have turned and sought despair as consolation
          or agony's cessation,
I surrendered or thought I surrendered forever,
          drawing the shades
Which shut out the blue rivers of morning, ending
          my vigil,
Telling myself that the self was nothing, and all was
          nothingness,
Nature was nothingness, and desire was nothing but
          passage,
The passage from darkness to nothingness to dark
          nothingness.

— *Then* I was almost glad that it was thus, thinking
                    it must be thus,
Thinking that all my other thoughts had been (how else
                    must it seem, might it seem, must it be
                    to most of us?)
Deceptions, illusions, delusions, satanic imaginations,
                    hideous
                    In the end, as the snake-like convolutions
                    of the brain
                    Which were the source and force of
                    hallucination.
And I knew the rise and the return after the failure
                    and the fall.
I knew and now I know the tone and the chant of rapture,
                    supreme and surpassing all, of the lost,
                    saved, the jubilee of those having
                    awakened from the dream
                    by the dream's conclusion.

Placidly at dusk — in hushed serenity
The hushed serene
Arose above the green
The waters were choirs wherein the sunlight chanted
The silence of space was a great blue balloon
Mounted aloft, waiting and attentive
The great blue bell, the dome which holds
                    The daylight and the night
The noon of turquoise diamonds diamonding
                    and gold golding
                    and radiance entranced and ringing
               dancing in all the kinds of lances. . . .

. . . Thou art confessed!
The roots of riverhood
                    are not in rain!

A brass of gleaming,
A pewter reticence,
A lucency, a transparency
The passing shows of
                plangent passions . . . starlings,
                star-winged
                starwings
Tapered.

. . . Were there lovers before me? How could there be
    since I
Discovered the self or — to insist again —
Invented it, by staring in a glass
And misconceiving the image of my face:
Of those who have fallen in love since then,
[*missing lines*]

The river possesses and continually blesses
Dreams of the sky in many disguises,
The sessions of its processions discover
All glittering radiance within the exaltation
Of the visual and visible imagination!

Under the meadows of the milky way
Under the marvels of the marble blue
The faint and bonewhite moonlight, faintly shining,
Seemed and sustained the mystery, or apparition
Glimpsed and guessed all day in the sun's glory,
And all the stories
Rippled and sparkled momentarily to me
— For first, I thought, the flowers existed only
In the contemplation of the stars. And then

The stars became the petals of the flowers
Of powers hidden, infinite and generous,
Flowing over, overflowing in boundless plenitude,
Possessing and possessed, blessing and blessed —
All luxury, fulfillment and largesse.
The river's coat — which half-concealed and half-revealed
The curves of sleekness, the slopes of suppleness
As the current rode and flowed, promised a tenderness
My face attracted, and an allure which promised me . . .

The river sang again of truth's variety,
Which is the light's plurality and ingenuity.
Lighting up, and misleading if too long believed.
            The light
Lolling upon the river's flow, descanted
On how all things are magnified and multiplied,
How emulation is an exaltation. The trees
Became a grove, a slowly curving orchard,
The river's tree became the harp, immense,
    of goddesses.
The river sang and said:
Death is not a spectacle or a catastrophe,
It is a distant eminence, far off, powerless, same as a point
    of view,
            Having nothing to do with love and victory
Nor with Dionysus, nor Apollo . . .
Phoenix fulfillment and fatherhood
Are other and otherwise to be understood.

— The poet is a shepherd of being,
The poet is the one who keeps the archives of the stones,
And makes immortal the lady among the rocks
And is the crying of the rocks, and draws in his flocks
To the fortitude of the acceptance of experience.

Another's face allure and desire, fixed on me,
And that was why I looked and looked,
Was why the others laughed until they shook,
Rollicking, looking into their own
Perfected self-deception, dark and sweet as the bone.

— Other than all the others and my self
            The river was
Sleekness and silk and supple,
            — The infinite blue above became, I saw,
Tender and infinite —
            An arch, contained yet magnified, within the flow,
Curving and curved, upon the river's face
The beauties of the stream supported my utmost dream!

A simple door opens upon an abyss . . .

Commanded reality, or uncommanded?
When I stare with much desire, my face becomes
A squint, a frown, and something falsified by hope,
Impatience, eagerness: and what I see
Is neither what I desire nor what is there:
My grasping gaze seizes what is a blur
And makes a hybrid of the blur and my desire,
A fiction and distortion of the uniqueness of reality.

Art thou not fortunate? Hast thou not seen
The foetus-like, the hideous, the obscene?
Yet equally, the admirable and the beautiful
In the leaves, darkened, but glittering and green
Within the river's glass fallen but supernatural —

. . . My faces were my apes: my apes became
Idolatrous . . .

. . . The sunlight became a jubilee of canaries:
Its genius engendered fury upon fury of blaze,
And then the beating of great wings began, the eagles rose
Above the orchards where the apples fattening and burned,
   burned.
From plump green to rounded red . . .
And I was lifted far above the hope and dread of love, above
The will and pounce of the chicken hawks, the willow of
   the dove.
Then love was but the door of mystery.
It was no more the terror beyond all mastery,
And ceased to be the midnight's leaping mystery.

I heard:
"The engine sighed softly,"
I listened to the machine's persistent drone, moan
"He commanded real fear,"
And felt the stage fright of guilt
The sweat of sympathy . . .

                : death to apes

The gods demanded, required, commanded
Instead of a cock, a pigeon,
a dog, a goat, or a pig,
The sacrifice of a culprit, a cupid.

"She ruffled the cards: she shuffled them
        She shuffled them agayne,
Those who deserve to die,
Die the death they deserve,"

Drums: white drums: the white round drums
Of the slowly swaying buttocks of drunken girls.

(*1958*)

IV

Kilroy's Carnival
A POETIC PROLOGUE FOR TV

Prologue: Night One

A Disc Jockey (*broadcasting anonymous: nothing but his voice is heard: nothing is seen*):

It is midnight now, it is very still: dusk and silence on all the dials from coast to coast, the darkest hour — of the heart — before the first morning, for now the air is hushed and empty. This is the farthest hour from the moment when the cocks take fire and in choir salute *l'élan en vitale,* the energy that moves the sun and the other stars, bursting and chanting in roaring braggadocio: The heart has its reasons which reason cannot understand, and the mind has its desires which the heart cannot bear, has aspirations with which the heart cannot contend; because the mind is its own place, grace and power.

Then at dawn the sun's blaze describes the meaning of astonishment, the leaves in the trees and the birds among the leaves, sign and sigh, being far beyond the being which doubts and believes:

"The darkling night has suffered death, has perished before the face and blaze of the primal fire! Morning, the dearest, begins to mount. Day, the deathless, arises again! Kiss me, daylight. Feather me all over with the warmth of light and the light of warmth!"

And the birds chirrup, cherubic, lipping and dripping, in twitter and chortle, whistle and bubble. Their calls and their cries are little and lyrical, declaring that every fowl is a phoenix! every bird is a word! (and every word is a bird!) Every day is a birthday! Every child is a ghost reborn at dawn!

And in the world of the heart and in the heart of the world every ghost awaits resurrection in the womb of the darkness.

85

And the chicken hawk, death, who hovers over us, is Elijah's raven: bearing us the manna of darkness! and the trees confess that they are harps of the leafy green-ness. And the bantam cocks cry: "Pride: stud is power."

And the orchard is a kindergarten and singing school for flying sopranos in the east of morning's jubilee, in the boughs of the apple tree of the world.

And the rooster roars Hallelujah, and the distant cocks reply Hosannah! and in the depths of the body's tyranny and the dream's lunacy, the sleeping who still possess the power of laughter are quickened by the hurrahing of dawn's demagogues, morning's fanatics. Intimations of the morning's growing glory haunt them, hinting in a delicate whiteness which touches their eyelids tenderly, softly. Then their hearts canter and romp like colts playing; and the hills, the woodlands, the lounging body of this life, this death, murmur a hymnal:

"Summer is the secret: summer is eternal, before the summer, summer is coming; after summer ascends in the maize and the wheat and descends in the heavy fruit and brittle leaf summer turns away that it may return, it falls to rise and dies that it may return in the fullness of its green glory, the irresistible triumph of trees in full flowering. The heart has its season, before and beyond reason, summer is the heart's reason which reason cannot comprehend and cannot begin or end."

... An interruption. These interruptions — as those of you know who are not merely sick and disturbed tonight only and separated tonight only from the magic and the magnetism of sleep's divinity — are characteristic and unavoidable; inoffensive after a week, and often desirable; admirable, at times, far more original than the queries which arise in normal consciousness. I will now read from them at random:

The question is: "Who did you vote for in the national election of 1952?" Signed, Mark Hanna. The answer, Dear

Mark Hanna, Tweed of Ohio, Cleveland's first Richelieu, is simple: "I like I.Q." This is what my house cat remarked after regarding long and wistfully the two leading candidates on TV.

Question two: "How about some music?" Signed, "A Savage Beast." Dear Canine, You have had music, the music of language. And there is music everywhere in the air, if you care to tune in. But if your request is literal — an extremely improbable possibility — you need only switch on your phonograph and listen to your master's voice, dear Savage Canine, dog in the manger.

Question three: "What team won the World Series in 1914?" Signed, Forgetful. Postscript: "What horse won the Kentucky Derby in 1939?"

The answer to your first question, Forgetful, is, The St. Louis Blues. The answer to your postcript question is, Hallucination, a nightmare, won the Kentucky Derby on the first of September, 1939. The famous classic took place on the Polish Border.

Question four: "Do you have a sense of humor?" Signed, Smiles. Dear Smiles, It would be ungracious of me to answer since any answer would surely displease you. I might say, "Yes: Do you know any jokes?" Or I might question you and ask: "Does your wife have a smiling face which resembles your mother's smiling face? If not, why not?" It would be incest to answer yes or no, yet if you did not, you would have to hide or reply: "Are you afraid? What are you afraid of, Smiles?"

Question five: "What is a monologue?" Signed, Hard of Hearing. Dear Hard of Hearing, A monologue is a log that has lost its jam. Jam you, Disingenuous: if you ask rhetorical questions, you must expect ridiculous answers. You are, I am sorry to say, either disingenuous or self-deceived — the latter is more to be feared — The truth is that you are the one who wants to do all the talking.

Question six: "Was your mother a virgin at the time she embraced monotony?" Signed, Vivacious. Dear Vivacious,

My mother has preserved her spiritual and emotional virginity to this very hour, and surely will not abandon herself at this point or in the future. I was conceived in a dream that she was dancing the Hesitation Waltz in Jersey City with the life of the party. She gave birth to me in a state of dudgeon and savage indignation and has insisted ever since that I am the foal of soul slander, a libelous accusation, a malignant growth. I will not elaborate on this point or comment on her attitude toward the ambiguous scion she has ever denied or regretted, except to say that, in short, she has accused me of celebrating Mother's Day, Ash Wednesday, Yom Kippur, and Good Friday the very same twenty-four hours of contrition and atonement.

Question seven: "Do you believe in going the limit prior to the nuptials, or companionate marriage?" Signed Bias. Dear Bias, You are sitting on your answer. Some time fairly soon we shall deal with the subject of love directly. For the time being, let me add only this brief message: Promiscuity is just around the corner — of the eye. We will now pause for station identification, trivial and misleading: and then we will hear a few words from our monster, insidious, acquisitive. Time marches on, time staggers forward.

MR. SINGER (*the announcer*):

This is Station WXYZ, friends of the listening audience. You have been hearing the voice of our midnight-to-morning disc jockey, Orville Wright, Jr., in his characteristic and highly original — some would say extremely personal and at times offensive — conversational style: his mastery of repartee has quickly made him a very popular nightly favorite. What is more, his tendency to give himself to description, intense in emotion and high-flown in tone — which has been viewed with mixed feelings by most of you — some say he is too poetic, some say he is a piercing bore — has, however, captured and fascinated a gentleman who wishes to remain anonymous — save for the fact that he has endowed Mr. Wright with unlimited funds to say whatever comes to mind whenever it does. Hence we take pride and pleasure in being able to tell you that this is no longer a sustaining program. Mr. Wright now has *carte blanche:* freedom of speech and the backing of millions. Tomorrow night there will be a special announcement concerning a contest which Mr. Wright has decided to run on his program, a contest suggested by various quiz programs all over the nation. We now return to Mr. Wright himself: tonight he will continue as he has in the past, and in a moment you will hear his summary of the latest developments in the news of the world.

ORVILLE:

Charming news from near and far. The capitals of Europe predict that there will be a cold war all summer long. Physicists and astronomers plan to play atomic ping-pong at Princeton soon. Mr. Frank Costello has told the press that crime does not pay. Marlon Brando declared yesterday that he no more needs Hollywood than a moose needs a hatrack. He added that, if as rumor hath it, Marilyn Monroe parlays Grushenka, a róle she has requested, in "The Brothers Karamazov," he intends to join Ringling Brothers as a Bearded Lady.

However.

This was a normal day, as days in the fearful twentieth century go; the number of rapes, seductions, murders, and perjuries were average. Intellectuals were eggheads, pearls were cast to swine. Rain fell. Sparks flew. Dust rose. Quiz kids were questioned. Night followed day as day will surely follow night. But, above all — most important of all even and most ignored, the Creation occurred. To those who have tuned in for the first time, I must say as I have said before: the Creation occurs every morning at dawn and all day long. The world is a fire, a great fire, a bonfire, a wild fire, a conflagration: it must be sustained by a new supply of fuel continually. So it is appropriate to draw again upon incidents and view on that very first day when God made heaven and earth. Many were the comments, then as now, some angels snickered, some remained preoccupied; others were suspicious, still others, it should be needless to say, were conservatives: they felt no change was necessary or justified the unavoidable risk.

During the first day and in the fading light of the first dusk, there were a variety of cheers and sneers, mocking exclamations, and dumfounded admiration, spoken carefully or carelessly, sincerely or politely, candidly or cautiously, by angels beholding the spectacle.

ORVILLE:
And now to conclude the portion of tonight's program which has to do with the comments of the angelic orders as they looked down upon the Creation:

— A Stunt. A tour de force. A gross and grotesque exaggeration.

— Elohim has gone too far.

— The world's a great success: colossal, a masterpiece!

— Begin with animals, end up with a zoo. Start with a jungle, end up with a circus.

— This is a violation of the laws of nature.

— Now we will all have to work six days a week.

— I just can't wait to get Lucifer's point of view on all this.

— It's all quite irritating and depressing. Were cockroaches and mosquitoes really required either now, or in the fullness of time?

— I have regarded developments with some interest, tinged, I will not deny, by doubt and anxiety.

— Why was it not possible to leave well enough alone?

— Let there be light means let there be night also: Thus it is in all, in all things newly invented: The winner is the loser and success is failure.

Now let us hear a lyric which may or may not be appropriate:

A Popular Score

O Nirvana
Don't you wait for me
I'm going with Mañana
She's the only girl for me.

I don't want Miss America,
I don't want Miss Paree,
My girl is Miss Utopia,
We're going steadily.

I don't want the boss's daughter,
She might be a wife-in-law,
And say her father bought her
A fortune-hunting bore!

So get along Nirvana,
I've fallen for Mañana,
She's my only marijuana
She's the only bride for me.

From here out to Montana
From here to Caroline
There's only one Mañana,
Mañana shall be mine!

I'm all through with plurality,
I have a blind date with reality,
We're going steadily:
So get along Nirvana,
My girl is sweet Mañana
She's the only hope for me.

ORVILLE: (*Broadcasting again, at an hour long after midnight, and not long before morning. He speaks as one who is rehearsing in solitude, perhaps before a small looking-glass. But again only his voice is heard: nothing is seen*):

A throne exclaimed: Wow!

A Power snickered: Anything for a laugh!

A Domination remarked: This is pure virtuosity!

Several said: We were not consulted. Some maintained that the angelic orders had been insulted. Two insisted it was all a flash in the pan. Another asserted with scorn and contempt: If this had been necessary, it would have come into existence a long time before now.

One angel remarked: This is remarkable. Whatever our ultimate judgment may be, this is remarkably remarkable. Extraordinary!

And here, at random, at seeming random, are some of the other angelic comments:

— What's the big idea?

— Too early to tell.

— Let's wait and see.

— Well: blow my horn!

— This is the beginning of the end.

— Personally I have always detested practical jokes for one and only one reason: they are unamusing.

— Let's be fair and reserve judgment.

— I see no need for alligators.

— Mark my words: this will come to no good.

— I see no reason for all the excitement.

— All aboard for Armageddon! Pandemonium, here we come.

— It hardly seems worth all the trouble.

— What does he have in mind? What next? What now? Now anything can happen and sooner or later — just you wait and see! — anything and everything will happen!

— We are going to be accused of being responsible for anything that goes wrong.

— Everything was so pleasant until this big production came along.

— This is one of those things, like sledding, which are easier to start than to stop.

— The [*word missing*] does not appear to be aware that he is playing with dynamite!

— Invention is the mother of dissension, the midwife of contention.

— Yes, we have no bananas.

That is all, for the morning, on the subject of the Creation, and all the wise and foolish versions thereof.

We will now hear a few words from our lobster.

AN ANNOUNCER (*A recorded voice, different from that of Orville Wright, but not too different and stylized so that it will suggest that it is Orville himself, shifting to parody and satirical ventriloquism*):

Money talks: and what does money say? Glugg: glugg: glugg. I must have my way or I won't pay. This is the language of desire and fear, which may be translated thus: Money talks: and what does it say? Give me what I want, if you want me to pay. This is your announcer, Cash Howells, thanking you for listening and returning you to our studio, and to Mr. Orville Wright's all-night program. Silence and blackness are over the land of the new world, the night of the darkness after midnight, resembling the void before the first day of Creation:

It is very still, and the silence resembles the boredom of the Sahara, the deathly silence of rocks. This is the last hour before the first morning. All the magic powers of the earth and air rest, hushed and acquiesce to the night's pantomime of the abyss of nothingness.

And I, who remain faceless as a wall, am a disc jockey rhetorical as a storming sea, riding the channels and the waves of the night after midnight, which is a long tunnel, a sepulchre, a pyramid, black or lighted, marble as the blue and as empty and deceptive. . . .

Let us freely admit that the waking are waiting — they lean forward little unknowingly to the vast vagueness of the darkened world even as the sleepers shiver a little in ripples of unrest as the delicate clearness and dearness of morning nears.

One who listened throughout last night wrote this question: "Are you a conscientious objector to life like the inspired novelist Count Leo Tolstoy?"

The answer is that I am conducting an interminable filibuster against the death of the heart in the little death of each day. Do you understand the reason and the reasons that you were and are sleepless? How often I find it necessary to say to myself: Give us this day our little death that we may possess like Lazarus and winter the experience of the phoenix.

Too much coffee, too much tobacco! Too much hope, too little patience: when desire becomes so passionate that it is an uncontrollable disconnected comet, chariot and runaway juggernaut. Then each sleepless one must ask: "Where am I? Are the reports of the five senses to be trusted very often? For the eye declares: the earth is flat: the sun rises and descends in the sky all day, and in all abundance and all green vividness summer denies the reality of winter."

Thus the wakeful wonder and wander. But now the divinity of sleep is the river of enchantment in which all other souls are anchored. And it is more still than the throats of the guilty when they first come upon hopelessness and eternity, eternal hopelessness: and have said in their hearts: "Hopelessness is eternity. Eternity is hopeless."

And now I begin again, a disc jockey who has ridden the nightmare of history in the Armageddon Derby, a steeplechase rider of the abyss, here the heart of darkness is an apocalypse-like volcano, erupting. . . . This is where I begin, here where it is forever three o'clock in the morning in the depths of the heart and of the night of North America: anxiety is diastole, desperation is systole, yin and yang are in or out, they swing and sway, squeezing the heart's accordion:

the blare comes forth from the bagpipes crying to Roland: too late! too late! Roncesvalles is lost in the past.

and the flutes chant: the beauty of morning passes like a flash of lightning!

the beauty of puberty is everyman's Pocohontas!

the beauty of youth is everyman's Eurydice!

the beauty of beauty is as blind as love.

At night, in the blindness of sleep, every man's son is Absolom. The days of youth are Circe's swindle. The princes of morning are the henchmen of Lucifer, the gangsters of Satan. And love becomes a Roman candle enacted in darkness, and less, very often — a firefly's sparkle.

It is true, again, in the stupor of sleep, all night that the life of man resembles the moment of lightning of a flashlight photograph: or it is as the sudden erratic tree of lightning, making all things for an instant ghastly:

As heart cries unto heart, and the heart, sentenced to the penal solitude of consciousness, hears only the howling of jackals, the mewing of gulls, above a barren coast, and after a time hears only the wind's answer: which is as the crying of rocks.

Then the heart says to itself: nothing is ever enough: too much is never enough: love is ever unsatisfied: every child is a shot in the dark, a billion-to-one shot.

We have worshiped Apollo and pinned all our hopes on a foetus repugnant and bug-eyed as a frog or a gas-mask.

We have placed all our eggs in a basket over the abyss of tomorrow.

We have wagered fountains of fond desires of the heart on the roulette wheel of history,

Lord have mercy upon us:

And may the Future have mercy upon us,

Love have mercy upon us,

O hope, let us depart at last from your mountains, the heights of anxiety, the cliffs of vertigo, the pits of despair.

The captains and kings have cried to hope and love and freedom of the heart: "Let our people go." The princes and premiers have pleaded with love also: "Let our people go: let them depart from the tyranny of the freedom of the kingdom of the heart: which is within us."

And now, for relief, variety, a change of key, a change of tone, I recite an anthem by Calderón:

We live while we see the sun
Where living and dreams are one.
And living has taught me merely this:
Man dreams the life that he is
Until life's dream is undone.
The king dreams that he is a king!
(— Stop! stop! what a thing to say:
Whether in earnest or in play —)

And all the praise he receives
Is written in the wind and the leaves,
Or in frost streaked upon the pane
Or in the dribbling of the rain;
It is dust and not laurel or bay
When death ends all in a breath:

Where, then, is the pomp of a throne?
It perishes sooner than the bone.
In the other dream which is death
Man dreams whatever he may be
And no man knows his own dream:
As I, too, dream and behold

That I dream, dreaming that all pain
Is a blessing disguised, and untold.

What is life? A tale poorly told?
What is life? Images which seem
The reality at the end of a dream!
The greatest of all good is small:
The belief that life is a dream
And that is all that it is: all!

(Silence for a few seconds; a sigh as of one who is almost exhausted; the rustle of papers, the tearing open of envelopes.)

MR. SINGER:
Mr. Wright has interrupted himself in order to read the messages which have just arrived in the studio. He will return, shortly, and attempt to answer them. Meanwhile, while we wait, we will try to bring up to date those of you who have only recently listened to this midnight-to-morning program. Judging by previous inquiries, the majority of listeners are curious and want to know more about Mr. Wright himself: his background, education, and other vital statistics. Although Mr. Wright has nothing to conceal, he has asked that these questions be answered as he has already answered them. He has said, from time to time, and I quote, "I am a graduate of several institutions of higher learning, a student of the electoral college, and of the mystery of history; from time to time, I have been an announcer, bouncer, denouncer, pronouncer, and pollster: the underlying unity of purpose in these dispersed occupations and preoccupations has been my infinite interest in — to be brief — the American Dream."

And here now is a summary of Mr. Wright's answers to questions about such related subjects as the state of the union, the promise of American life, the probable future. Questioned as to what the population of the United States of America would be in the year 2000, he answered: Increasing. When asked to elaborate, he replied with a like terseness: there will be no pubs in the public library, then as now; there will be more trees than poems, more books than readers, more students than teachers, more fools than schools, and opportunity will continue to contend and compete with opportunism. Only the hopeless optimist will be a bigamist, none but the lonely heart will be the life of the party.

"Then as now, the bankbook will be the most popular of all books, and the checkbook will be second, among best sellers. As it is, it shall be: Canadian Club will be preferred to the Book of the Month Club, there will be Pindars and Pandars; there will be bores and whores, charmers and farmers, gold hearts and hearts of gold, monogamy and monotony will be at times mistaken for each other, hearts will seek flowers, love will be blind, justice will need glasses, the tree of technology will put forth more leaves of absence.

"And again, as before, the present will be the future. Then as now, a Daniel will come to judgment, and whether he is named Honest Abe or Mahatma Gandhi, he will stand a good chance of being assassinated: again and again the scapeghost will be sacrificed, new truths will be viewed as implausible, shocking, and outrageous, and Pegasus, a dark horse, will win the Preakness in the warm May darkness of the mind and the heart.

"The FBI will capture IOU, SOS, and AWOL. Wall Street will fall like the walls of Jericho and Niagara Falls will rise again like a geyser, a gusher; Time will ride again, as before; and the four horsemen will be seen riding in the distance, at the horizon; there will be war and peace, peace and war; there will be intense hope and intense despair, love and suicide, birth and death, illusion and disillusion, dream and awakening, a beginning and an ending; continually.

"Nevertheless! nevertheless! the more it is the same, the more it will be different; the more generic, the more unique; there will be nothing except the new under the sun with each new morning, nothing will be more beautiful than the morning except for the mornings to come, nothing will be so abundant in promise as the future: hope, ambition, and love will be heartbreaking, then as now. It will be clearer and clearer that Columbus discovered not only America but Hollywood. The moon pictures will still be transparent revisions and paraphrases of the American Dream.

"There will be more scapegoats than goats, then as now. It will be said that again or for the first time: Gentlemen prefer bonds; a rolling stone will gather no remorse: Go rest, young man, go rest; let him who is without sin go out and get stoned." We return you now to Mr. Orville Wright, Jr.

ORVILLE:

I turn now to the letters which have been written tonight: let me say again, as I will have to say henceforward, that my comments must not discourage you from sending communications of any kind or temper. They will always be welcome.

Here is a letter which interests me very much, as you will see:

"You are a nut: a complete nut: that's why your program keeps becoming more and more popular. I am sorry for you, but far more sorry for these listeners who like your crackpot comments and comedy: it makes them feel superior! They become smug about their barbaric ignorance, which tends, at other times, to trouble them vaguely. They are soothed by your erratic chattering, charged by your evasion of logical sequence, restored to the cold peace of ordinary consciousness by your freedom and wantonness in skirting and skipping the rational order of intelligent discourse.

"In the depths of their minds and hearts they listen to you and feel: maybe I am not at all that I might be, should be, would like to be, could be, but at least I am not a screwball: I am not a nut.

(Signed) Annoyed."

(*Pause*). ORVILLE:

I pause a moment for the dignity and the courtesy of silence.

Dear Annoyed, Thank you very much: I am truly grateful. Silence is often the foul fen of disease, soft and rotten. Silence is often fury (perhaps you are, in fact, furious — you certainly are more irritated than annoyed: but, it must be said again, nothing is more desirable than candor: my expression of gratitude is entirely sincere.

I repeat for those of you who have just tuned in, the burden of the message from Mr. Annoyed, our compatriot in hope and aspiration, is: "You are a nut: a complete nut." And I answer, not in antipathy, but in the fullness of sympathy:

Are you preoccupied with nuts? If you are, why? Is your excitement or, at any rate, extreme sensitivity, a form of obsession or of fear?

Here is still another letter, different indeed from the two which preceded it:

"You said that your chief theme was the dream within a dream within a dream, the dream of the new world forever new, the dream of deathless hope ever renewed, reborn each morning and after each fiery death as the phoenix and the springtide. How do we know that this is not a delusion or a hoax, a teapot tempest, a con man's swindle, a crackpot's delusion? Don't forget that you yourself said that the entire history of the United States of America was made possible by an error in navigation, the lifelong delusion of a destitute optimist, seeking sesame, intent on finding a passage to the

Indies and unable to tell a coral reef from a continent, incapable of distinguishing between a harbor and a hole in the ground. The discoverer of America was the kind of a mariner — you know this is true — who, trusted to pilot the Staten Island Ferry, would land in Far Rockaway and announce that he had dropped anchor in the port of Utopia: he was incompetent and hallucinated: looking for a haystack, he would have found a needle: looking for a needle, he would have found a haystack.

Admit that I am right? Was Columbus capable of guiding a lily cup from one end to another of a moving railroad coach? And if the new world was discovered through hallucination, is it not also clearly true that a tea party was the first move toward independent sovereignty: a tea party to protest against an acutely resented tax: and no one now remembers that the founding fathers of this country were Danton, Robespierre and Napoleon Bonaparte.

(1958)

101

V

Previously Uncollected Poems

Poem to Johann Sebastian Bach

(For Julian)

Out of the watercolored windows, when you look,
Each is but each, and plain to see, not deep:
So does the neat print in an actual book,
Marching as if to true conclusion, keep
The illimitable blue immensely overhead
And the night, night of the living and the dead.

Brother and brother, of one Father,
Near and clear and far,
How indeed we mistake each other.
Despair, and fear, and care.

I drive in an auto all night long to reach
That place where all wheels grip no place and cease,
I never end the turning world, the breach
Where no spring is, nor winter is, but peace:
The only absolute stillness is the frieze
Of the escalator where the damned crowds rise.

Brother and brother, of one Father,
Near, and clear, and far,
How, afterward, we will know each other.
Beware, and share, and care.

(1934)

105

Poem for Jacques Maritain and Leon Trotzky

The Gentile night and the white stars in congress
Still the traffic's racked energy;
And the hurdy-gurdy newsreel of memory
Flashes the past in its stilted sadness,

Standing on what brink then? By my room's window,
Thinking of the sources of situation
—Of the people's confrontation
When they see themselves dirty in another's shadow!

O Marxist drunk at the teats of Tiresias,
Is night still close to morning? Will the morning
Once more from rumorous darkness release us?

Tonight is more than night and more than meaning.
Stars are the buds of morning, do you know?
Look, in the West, at the white moon dreaming of snow.

(n.d.)

The Maxims of Sisyphus

(Sisyphus' Success)

Although I was tenacious, I never learned
  the wisdom and will of tenacity;
Although I was persistent, and praised for persistence,
At first faint falling off of inspiration's desire
  the black hood of despondency covered my face,
  fell over it
To till and toil and delve and dig, dumb in the darkness
  chinning and clutching, darkened and weakened
I never knew until . . . nor knew how the piddling puddling
  persistent will is the perpetual way,
  the royal real route to the richest fulfillment.

. . . Persistent, but faint of heart, passionate and
  yet apathetic,
  How often I turned my face away,
  How often avoided unpleasant imperfection,
  squeamish and absolute, and did not run up against
  the taboo abomination, but ran away and ran back.
  Running away instead of running running through
How could I perceive how often success was won after
  many repeated Sisyphean failures
  (When I often had been drunken with the romance
  and fortune of spontaneity, when often the more
  the effort, the worse the denial or outcome or . . .
  When all that I most wanted was near as my hands
  and feet, and had been, ever. . . .

(1954)

107

How Can He Possess

How can he possess
The dreams and extremes of hope and despair . . .
(which are named Death and Morning)?

He must wish to dance at everyone's wedding.
He must wish to be everyone and everything.
He must be a Trappist, but eloquent as Trotzky,

Chaste but a gigolo,
the Czar yet Figaro.

Hence how can he be anything but nothing or zero
If this *dramatis personae* is ever a necessity?

(n.d.)

Sonnet

I follow thought and what the world announces
I lean to hear, and leaning too far over,
Fall, and babied by confusion, cover
Myself in drowse, too tired by such bounces.
But in sleep are dreams across zigzagging snow
Descending quietly and slow, like minutes,
And on this peace the soul again begins its
Rhetoric of desire, older than Jericho,
And rails once more, like birds of early morning
Urchinous on branches and like newsboys,
"Extra, this is the meaning of life,
Here is the real good, beyond all turning,"
Till night goes home, astonished by such cries,
I wake up, and, to feel superior, I laugh.

(1938)

The Power and Glory of Language

Lordly and mighty language—eagle of time and space,
Giving to the mind the possession and freedom of both,
Touring and traveling in the ancient whiteness
    and blueness,
Sailing in the winedark of Greece and olive green
    Mediterranean,
Seeking cinnamon and wisdom in the Orient's scriptures,
Harking to and holding the whistle of birds and lisping
Of infants and the joshing and jargon of boys, the squawk
And the yelp, the echo and the innuendo and belly-laugh,
Giggle, horse-laugh, titter, and snicker, containing
The midnight of meaning and the lightning of insight,
The small stars of the perception of white flowers
And falling flakes, the fingertip and the city, the continent
Of love, the first flush of Eros and the plunging delirium
(Which is a dying and a little death), her unbearable ecstasy
Began, the pulse and gong clamored and hammered,
She whimpered with pleasure, she sobbed in the procession
Of passion, she slid down the valley of the fury of joy
On skis which soared as she fell . . .

What have they called the little girl? Perdita, Judith, Marina?
The grace of language, which is the living ghost and holy
    spirit
Of joy (because it is unseen, it is gifted with wings,
    and is small enough and powerful enough to be all things),
It is a bond and a meeting place
It is a currency which passes all borders
And proceeds through all nations,

110

It is given to all who take it
It is aristocratic as well as democratic.

(n.d.)

The Sequel, the Conclusion,
the Endlessness

For thus, since the body's death is quick, seems less,
Consoled or hidden by unconsciousness,
While every little death lies sprawling and awake
In the sleepless glade of consciousness,
Therefore the body's death seems the liberty
Of nothingness, the dream of every suicide,
Criminal, and tyrant, afraid of each little death,
Or sickened by the terror of new hope,
Or certain, again, that every death of any hope
Concludes all hope and makes the body's death
More desirable than the recurrent torment of the years
Of life with a dead heart and pathos instead of hope:
Or hope that hope may be reborn once more
Only to be disappointed as before:
This is the ignorant bigotry of all despair:
This is the Utopia of all suicide.

The final dream of liberty we believe
And suicides seek with certainty
Is also their first vision of reality:
If it is true, it is not because either fear
Or crime are key to profundity and aware,
Revealing the heart of reality and the heart's reality.
For if they were, how would it be possible to start
The games which begin the hope and end in the death of
    hope,
the body's death, and the death of the heart?

(1958)

Poem: How Marvelous Man's Kind Is

When it is very dark, we see the stars clearly
—EMERSON

The universe is a machine for the making of gods
—BERGSON

How we marvel and must when most
Struggle to life and possess
That self or sense of the self
Which is either a hope or a myth
Shinnying the steeples of death
For the pigskin or fleece of pride!

If this passion did not exist
The captains and killers of wars
Surely would not persist
To their stone and pose;
And none would follow his dream
To the extremes of living and death:
Their soldiers, dreamstruck, enlist
Because they believe in a myth!

How we live! How we live by this!
Citizens of fantasy!
Pennants above an abyss
Limp, or blown stupidly.
As though the dream be true
Tomorrow in the country of the blue.

Now before we reach that shore
We are too sure or too unsure,
Fearing lunatic kings, or once more
Lunatics of intuitive doubt

—Caligula or Descartes!—
Till the truth of death do us part
From the stories and theatres of the heart.

(n.d.)

When I Remember the Advent

When I remember the advent of the dazzling beauty
  As it descended, sudden and unknown,
I turn again to stiffened stone, alone
  With the poverty of having known the dazzling of beauty,
But only as a memory is known, only as a lake,
  A weekend or midnight
Know the glory streaming the great blue heights
  Riding in a storm of white disorder
  The cavalry of Aurora Borealis.

(n.d.)

The Famous Resort in Late Autumn

The shouting of the sea and the storm storming
Was loud and louder, loud enough to waken the rocks
   & to shock
The stilt-borne salt-burnt spray-pocked creaking
   boardwalk
Which looking upon the ever-freshness of the unresting
foaming erupting ocean as an ancient crippled
   and exhausted old man
   gazing from the shore
As if the day and the summer and the carnival
   were no more
But only & forever the low and leaden night
Of the senseless sea struggling with the awakened rocks.

(1956)

He Who Excuses Himself
Also Accuses Himself

Listen, the dark lark chants once more
  Only the guilty are truly good!
A truth heartbreaking as war
  The penitent have understood.

Harken, how the demon once more sings
  As once, of love, to Socrates,
Or blesses the blankness of the snow,
  Since white is all colors, in disguise.

The dark bird whispers: *Have you understood
How only the guilty can be truly good?*

(n.d.)

117

To a Fugitive

The night you got away, I dreamed you rose
Out of the earth to lean on a young tree.
Then they were there, hulking the moon away,
The great dogs rooting, snuffing up the grass.
You raise a hand, hungry to hold your lips
Out of the waiting air; but lights begin
Spidering the ground; O they come closing in,
The beam searches your face like fingertips.

Hurry, Maguire, hammer the body down,
Crouch to the wall again, shackle the cold
Machine guns and the sheriff and the cars:
Divide the bright bars of the cornered bone,
Strip, run for it, break the last law, unfold,
Dart down the alley, race between the stars.

(n.d.)

118

Poem

        . . . window . . . winter . . .
The winter woods are wire and black
And by a vivid death possessed:
The orchard trees describe a rack
Upon the snow's blank vacant breast.
              . . . a shroud, a cloud, a lunar myth . . .
The trees' stripped lines writhe and arise
As in a Fury's passionate cry.
As if there were, beyond surprise,
A secret meaning in the sky!
              Is there? There is!
              Sure or perhaps?
              Sure as perhaps.
The pulse of being is faint and low
As the grey cloth of the snow sky:
The scene is true as summer's show,
The woods of winter are a lie
              true as most truths.

                      (n.d.)

Praise Is Traditional
and Appropriate

I loved the wood because I found in it
Mushrooms, berries, beetles, birds and other words,
Hedgehogs, squirrels, memories, quarrels,
   and the damp smell
Of dead leaves, and former lives.
               I reached the first barn
—where wheat was stored—halfway up the slope
   of the ravine
And saw her dancing, glancing twinkly eyes
Full of the hope and love which all thought mean,
And slate-green, slate-blue, blue or black like the sunrise
Skies, and in their variety and in their sheen
I thought that she was looking down at me
As if she understood past, present, and futurity.

(n.d.)

The Dances and the Dancers

All of us delight in dancing and in beholding dances:
  Some of us desire a horse ballet
    Great and heavy horses,
Percherons with limbs like heavy but supple sandbags
  Dragging and lumbering in an *Alla Tedesca*,
    and then, at the horse show, the cavalry of Vienna,
    and then the sleek race horses of Saratoga:

All of us delight in the formal dancing of others
  Because we are bursting with the force of uncontrollable
    desire:
    Hence, where there are horses, as where there are rivers
and skaters—*Virtuoisi* of the body's ebullience and deftness,
  By the spirit captured
    and trained to rapture.

Then there is a party of the city, the theatre and the school,
Then there is a dancing of the heart and the heart's birthday.
And even at the numbed peak of intensest winter cold
The skaters below the hill on the frozen lake
  or white courts,
Turn like the stars in free constellations
Under the blue; a cold shining, and seem more radiant
  and serene,
Than statues of the white goddess, Juno, the classic
    and imagined queen.

(n.d.)

121

Genesis

Selections from Book II

"Interpretation! that's the act of mind
Which we began, which now this sleepless boy
And from the very start that foreign voice,
Though intermittently except implicitly,
Have practiced with no little satisfaction—"

"It is the sunlight shining through the window,
It is the sunlight shining through the leaf
Showing as in analysis the veins—
It is the sunlight shining through stained glass,
Bringing rich colors to the ancient figures
Of the Bible tales which are the Western mind—"

"It is the preacher preaching on the text,
And with this act of mind, this pure sunlight,
Bringing fresh relevance to long-used words,
It is a man's reason travelling the world,
Just like the Wandering Jew, or Christ's good life,
Is is the 'essential Plato, he who saw
How the Idea is being,' genesis,
Motion, objective structure, all else vague!—"

"It is the teacher teaching in the classroom,
What the text means and how to take it in,
Whence rise the classics or the classroom books!
(Just like the preacher! just like the sunlight too!)
—Yet what, O sleepless boy, shall be replied
To those who say, interpretation's free,
Free and licentious, anyone can say

Just what he wants to say, Satan himself
Quotes scripture for all crime and each mind finds
What he brought with him, in the book or act?
What holds interpretation in its flight,
                    and makes it good or evil?
—O glory of the turning world! it is
The future whose events show true or false
Empty or relevant, senseless or sure
The inner structure and the inner future
Interpretation found in a book or act,
                         or thing. . . ."

"O New York boy, this is Life, Life in which
You cannot choose,
                    cannot create the world
No more than you can make a mountain lay
Without a valley!
                    O you might, in fact,
Spend years and millions filling up the gap
Which is the valley—
                    on and on and on,
Fill every mountain's every valley everywhere,
But in the end, all your accomplishment
Would be the levelling of mountains out
—No mountains anymore: thus your defeat;
Until the next quake broke your effort like
A house of playing cards!
                    brushed carelessly!
Let you then calm yourself! *Tais-toi*,
                         poor boy—
Pauvre enfant! Not to be Roman Stoic
And sink upon your sword like tragic heroes,
Not to be limp and lounge like sybarites,
Or those whom Dante saw, nor good nor evil,

Trimmers, he said, who made the great refusal—
Not to be flat with despair and effortless. . . .
—Yet! on the other hand not to do what
Your mother sometimes said for you to do
(Angry with you, unwilling to let you play
With all the other boys in city streets
After nine o'clock passed) 'Go knock your head
Against the wall!' she said when you, empty,
Asked her, 'What can I do Upstairs?

                              What can I do?'
Knock your head in the wall, she said to you!
O do not knock your head against The Great Wall
Of China or of Life: does not avail,
No less do the divinities ride through your head
Even as the street-car skates through it all night,
Piercing the after-midnight silence,

                              gnawing the rails and sleep,
With Industrialismus's pure means. . . ."

"O what a mess of judgment we have made,
Like many stricken birds they are arrayed!
The flying thoughts which from our last dismay
Issue like deathbed speeches, just as false,
A bit more hopeless, but as special too,
As different from the speech of every day
Passing as handkerchiefs and newspapers:
I too in the old life evaded all
By this or that device, like Hershey Green's
Telling the doctor that he's sick.

                              —A fresh start!
How that white paper freedom ruins the heart!
—Not to accept one's fault, but turn from it,
As if it never was, not to endure
One's imperfection as the very ground

Whence grows the fusing summer, full and green!
And to play new-born child or freshman thus
As if you washed with your blood your sins away:
This is the cowardice which is the first,
All else a mode of it, and not the glued
Flypaper which one cannot throw away,
Other retreats merely a piece of this—"

"All night, all this hardly bearable night,"
Said Hershey Green as to boring guests,
"No one but failures speak to me,
                                        did none
Of the dead succeed, or are they quiet now,
The great successful ones? and was there nothing
That with pure pleasure you remember when
You lived in the old life of hope deceived,
—Deception must itself have brought you joy—
I don't hear anything pleasant at all,
I don't hear one word which would help my hope,
Or at the very least, let it endure—"

"Sleepless Atlantic boy, what else would you
Expect? most men are failures and most men
Remember evil more than good,
                                        dead or alive!"

"Lo, we descend like light. Light. Light
Through the windowpane and through the eye,
Find out the private movements of the heart
And move with them. The hatred and the love
Color us, yet release us, like the scenes
Of the enacted play, in a like dark—"

So said a freshened voice, joyous,

Synoptic of the parts that the dead sung—

"Before the apartment house, set like a tomb
Among so many tombs, now, late at night
I hear the passing of an occasional car,
                         now and then, now and then,
On the Avenue. I hear the silence
                         like a wide sound,
Full of the ticking of hearts and clocks
                         in bedrooms and in lives—"

"Ah, if they were but wholly wholly there,
Contained in the body's box, separate from all
Divinities and all superior powers,
Free of the school, the street, the city, and the sea!"

"Great authors can become superior powers
And small divinities. As Spengler here,
So Machiavelli in the Renaissance,
Rousseau in the Enlightenment, Byron
Luther, Goethe, whose Werther killed young men
(Though they were fertile for the death he made):
O anything you see may be a cause,
Although elsewhere it is itself a thing:
Make the distinction! Any thing's old acts
Go on and on in time and place,
                         beyond its will,
Beyond its knowledge, overseas,
                         in the air,
Like the great lights and like the radio's voices,
There in the air although you cannot hear—"
"The causes moving in their many courses
Mix in a struggle whence each day arises—"

"As Adam named the beasts with careful love,
We name the animals and the divinities
Who walk about this newfoundland, America,—"
"As Socrates, who questioned everything
Because his love was great, we question all—"

"As Joseph, once I knew a sweet revenge
In basic psychological reviews,
Accused the innocents who perjured me,
Me innocent,
              showing sublimely then,
The justice who uncovers innocence,
Omniscient, generous, O all forgiving
And most successful brother who displays
How he was right throughout, in his conceit:
All dreams come true, and every feat performed!"

Hershey cried, "What has this to do with me?"

"A boy once died, and wandered through the scenes
He lived, saw them again, not living them
But *seeing* them, within their background,
                        ground and earth,
The flashback of the cinema,
                fadeout, dissolve, return. . . .
Wandered through memory's halls,
                    through all his life,
Saw what he lived and what he did not know,
Enjoyed and travelled through the whole of life,
Passionless, piteous,
              then he understood
And held the whole of life within his hands:
And you, O Hershey Green, who are not dead,
You may attain to this, go back to Life
If you have the strength!
             if your heart does not break:

Oh what a glory then,
                    patience and purity,
Labor in joy in knowing self-identity!"

"The sand upon the Red Sea shore, or on the beach,
Far Rockaway, where I admired the waves,
Pleased me because sterility and movement seemed
The sum of the green world . . .

"Nearer the city, the subway rises to the 'El,'
Comes to the stop called Gravesend, justly named,
Here in a huge cemetery wait the Judean dead
For that Redeemer other peoples have enjoyed,
                    katharsis or kingdom come,
                    fictive or true, who knows?
But anyway, *enjoyed*, except by those stiff-necked
                    poor and passionate folk
In whom I participate, though ignorantly,
                    under the threshold of attention
                    and in the heart of darkness
                    the very center of death,
After the long trek and track from Palestine—"

"The main thing: Atlantic boy, is to see Life,
To see it as a progress and waste of days,
                    that is, as a story,
In which are certain scenes which seem to show
                    all that was there a while,
The glittering attractions of dignity and pleasure. . . .

"The mind is the greatest tourist, never at home,
And hence freely we pass through the places where Life
                    has agreed or agonized,
So we go on, seldom satisfied even a while:

But when we think of that Consciousness which sees all,
When then our minds like larks at heaven's gate sing,
Sing on, sing out
       our endless memory and hope of all things!"

"Nothing is left unsaid, no shame forgiven!
Nothing that I escape in common pity,"
Cried Hershey Green,
                    "Who knows so much about me,
Yet does not let me fly from agony,
Except, like tortured men to convalesce
Before the rack once more is placed upon
His hands, his mind, his pride, his private parts!
—All of the sordor that my life has known,
Every disorder, together or alone!
I take my guilt! I know it very well:
Was *I* the only one like that? Do they,
Like me, rehearse it over and over again?
                    all of it, every shame?
Whether they do or not, *I wish to die!*"

"Now we are coming to the very end,
Though every end is but a new beginning!
Now we approach the consummation which
Fulfills and justifies this shameful story,
Until it must be justified again,
As human beings, however satisfied,
By dinner, come for breakfast, until lunch
Renews the process and prolongs the life,
                         the vanity!"

And yet, O New York boy, harsh as this is,
This is the way to knowledge and to power,
This is the way to knowledge and to freedom,
Though as the poet said, After such knowledge,
What forgiveness?

                              yet will you be forgiven,
Though you do not forgive yourself!
                                             This is
The way that you must live! By this attention,
The utter writer's concentrated gaze
On every kind of thing from fly to mountain,
On every living moment of the movement
Of the breathing hoping soul among
The great divinities which struggle with
His waning liberty in Time the darkness
                              before you die!

"Not God himself can quite destroy the Past!
What's his forgiveness then? All men, Macbeth!"
So cried the tortured boy, crying for death!

"'O Death, great captain, lift anchor!
                              it is time!'
And lift away this passionate ruined man:
This guilty boy show how *he* does not die,
This boy is but one act of his, in dying . . .
                              Will move with you!
This gulf, Atlantic boy, will move with you,
As Pascal and Baudelaire, henceforth—
You will fear Death as one fears a great height
Full of vague horror leading who knows where? . . . ."

"You will see the infinite at every window,
Desiring always insensibility,
Which is your wish throughout this shameful night . . .
—Across the depth of your nights, God's knowing hand
Will draw more nightmares, greater terror
                              and horror,
Without an exit and without conclusion—"

"Thus all is a gulf,—'action, desire, hope,'
Language and thought. Silence is under all,
Appalling and empty space surrounds you now:
You lie in the coffin of your character,
Trapped by each effort to escape from it,
Just like a fly caught in a treacherous sweet—"

"Everything happens in the mind of God—"

"We know O Lord, we know it very well,
Your Judgement is a righteous one always,
However monstrous to the human mind!"

                    "ever the silver cord is loosed!
                    ever the golden bowl broken!"

"The soul of every life is in your hand,
Your hand is full of righteousness and truth!
O pure and righteous Judge! blessed art Thou,
Who know our guilt, forgive and understand,
After Eternity's impatient wait,
When we have lived it all again,
                    how many times!
May we pass with some others through the Gate,
Whence all may see Thy Face and see enough!
Who hardly are yet sure that Thou Art, yes!
                    and not a dream!—"
"Free of all monstrous made divinity,
Faced with Your Face and with Your Matchless Face,
Patient at last with self-identity!"

"Now we approach the darkness of to-night!"

"Now we approach the recognition scene!

The scene of scenes: all has been recognition!
Lucid obscenely, of the human condition!"

"Hershey, you see the true sufficient cause:
Capitalismus fell and you fell with it!
Even as financiers,
                            leaping exactly
From office buildings,
                            images of their world!"

"But hope can tell more lies than fabulists,
The human mind can run away with light's
Velocity to Asia, America,
And to the future, even as you dreamed.
And you who think that what fell down will rise
Lie to yourself! Capitalismus rules—
But it is ruled by one Cause infinite
In might and strength!rld
                            in power and glory!
Everything happens in the mind of God!
This is what we have come to tell you now!"

"And you, O guilty boy, who with your freedom
Took to your heart the monstrous infamy,
Capitalismus, and made your fantasy
Equal to it, just like an office building,
Must bend and break before the only one,
                            my God!"

"I lie in the coffin of my character!"

"At last! the present darkness! all is known!
Of what the Past was! all its private parts
Have been *in principle* shown clear before you:

Your freedom and your guilt is the whole truth,
Sleepless Atlantic boy, son of two Noahs!
You and your guilt, you are your liberty,
Made of your years,
                    in Time the darkness,
                    Time the turning fire,
                        which brings the day and night—"

"Your act is chosen by your rich poor heart
Among the living dying stupid mindless
                            and strong divinities;
No matter what compulsion they enact:
Your act is yours, you are your liberty,
                        your self-identity!
—Here hearts are tried as gold is tried in fire!"

"An age is ended and an age begins!
This is New York in the year 1930,
This is the end of the world and the beginning,
For there where freedom breathes the empty air,
                            changing, shifting, burning
                        In Time the darkness,
                            Time the fire,
Beginning and conclusion every moment
Wait for the freedom which creates anew
All the divinities and all the freedom,
                    all the fathers and all the children!"

"All is forgiven when guilt is accepted
Like a hard task that must at last be done,
And all begins again amid your guilt
When you feel freedom heavy in your hands,
Heavy as the wide world! light as the air,
Breathed in at will by him who wills to breathe!"

"This is the empty knowledge Death can render,
Empty with freedom, heavy with your guilt—
Pride has performed, using its liberty,
Gaze at your guilt, your ego, and your pride,
The ego in the end destroys the world,
Like Nero! and destroys the loving brother,
Like Cain! and in the end comes to believe,
Just punishment, that nothing else exists!
Gaze at this guilt, this ego, and this pride!"

"O God, give me the strength, give me the power
To view myself with nausea and disgust,
True hope, knowledge of liberty,
Knowledge of guilt, of death,
                              of self-identity,
And recognition of the living world!
—But whose is that foreign voice? who knows it all?"

"He is the one you do not know, O boy!
The snow which haunts your mind is freedom's
                                        image,
And Super-Nature's perfect analogue,
Fallen from high upon the human city!"

"The dead who speak to you are always with you!
—Nothing is lost and everything is won—"

"This can only be the beginning of the world
Approaching!
              this can only be the morning!
Pure snow-like light shows at the fourth floor window:
I lie in the coffin of my character,
I rise with my coffin and my liberty,
I rise with my coffin, self-identity!"

"Everything happens in the mind of God!. . . ."